A GIFT FOR

_____

FROM

_____

DATE

_____

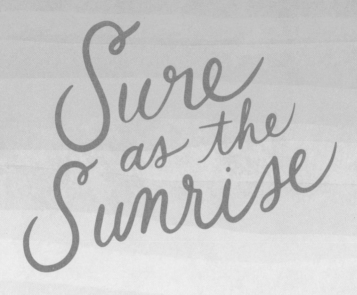

Sure as the Sunrise

100 MORNING MEDITATIONS ON GOD'S MERCY AND DELIGHT

EMILY LEY

THOMAS NELSON

Since 1798

Published in Nashville, Tennessee, by Thomas Nelson. Thomas Nelson is a registered trademark of HarperCollins Christian Publishing, Inc.

Thomas Nelson titles may be purchased in bulk for educational, business, fund-raising, or sales promotional use. For information, please email SpecialMarkets@ThomasNelson.com.

ISBN 978-1-4002-3131-7 (audiobook)
ISBN 978-1-4002-3130-0 (eBook)
ISBN 978-1-4002-3126-3 (HC)

Printed in China

22 23 24 25 26 DSC 10 9 8 7 6 5 4 3 2 1

To my dad, the original Early Bird. Thank you for being my guiding light and soft place to land. The size of your heart and the breadth of your humor are unmatched.

Contents

CONTENTS

CONTENTS

CONTENTS

Introduction

I've long been fascinated by the idea of a fresh start. By the jolt of joy found in a newly rearranged bedroom or the feeling of a new dress that fits just right. It's in the perfection of a recently cleaned kitchen, the bounce of a new haircut, and the crisp feel of the air on that day in October when the weather drops ten degrees and you know fall has arrived.

I crave that feeling daily: of newness, of happiness, of possibility. When the repetition of backpack packing, shoe tying, email answering, and laundry folding begins to make me feel stale, I crave the change of pace, the reminder I am still a girl wild at heart and an adventurer. When the responsibilities of adulting and mothering and homekeeping begin to feel extra heavy, I crave lightness, joy, and laughter. When the concerns of the world and of our fellow humans feel too complex to process, I crave truth and guidance, strong and steady. The feeling is not only electric, but it inspires action, movement, and growth. It's the perfect kick-start to a busy day, the perfect shift to nudge us back on track.

Reflecting on this feeling invites us to remember what it feels like to be deeply alive, to laugh with abandon, to seek out adventure, and to revel in delight. Even when our hair is weeks overdue for a new cut or the temperature is pushing 100 degrees, the feeling of hope brings us the perspective to believe that anything is possible and the knowledge that joy and delight surround us at every turn, if we pause long enough to see them.

I've learned that feeling of freshness, of renewal, and of joy can be found not only in rearranged spaces and day one of our new workout routine, but also when we slow down enough to savor the goodness the Lord has already given us, when we pause to reflect on the everyday magic already happening around us. It's in these ordinary moments that we best see God's love, mercy, forgiveness, grace, and steadiness.

Lord, let us use this daily practice of intention and reflection to know You better and to celebrate all You've given us to savor.

I woke one morning with the weight of the world on my chest. I hadn't slept well as it'd stormed much of the night before. The COVID-19 pandemic raged, virtual school was in full swing, and the busy season at work slowed to nothing. Like nearly everyone in mid-2020, I was afraid, overwhelmed, and lonely. I missed our extended family and friends, missed our school, missed our church. I grieved for what my children were missing of their childhoods. A fresh start seemed like a nice thought, but it was so far out of reach, I dared not consider the idea.

I took a deep breath and sat up, half-smiling as my daughter Caroline bounded into the room to tell me it was morning and she could now get out of her bed. I took her hand and slowly trudged to the living room, considering what the day would hold—likely a copy/paste from the day prior and the one before that—and counting the seconds until that first sip of coffee would be passing my lips. Everything felt hard.

God, did You forget us?

Looking up, I paused. What I saw out the glass doors that morning took my breath away. It wasn't the first sunrise I'd seen, but it was the first time God had clearly spoken to me through something so very ordinary.

As the sliver of bright, beautiful orange crested the edge of the water, just beginning to peek out and illuminate our world, I heard three words deep in my heart.

I didn't forget.

It was so clear and so poignant I felt my breath catch.

I didn't forget you. I didn't forget the sunrise. Don't miss this.

God brought the sun up that day. Just as He had thousands of times before. He didn't forget the task and He didn't forget us. We never have to wonder if He will bring the sun up in the morning. He brings it up with the same enthusiasm He had on that very first day. He didn't forget. He never has. He never will. Further, though occurring daily, it's no monotonous task for God.

As I watched the colors unfold and the sun begin to make its full appearance, I realized, this is actually a sacred, magnificent rhythm, an ordinary yet holy event. One I'd walked past a million times, without considering the magic within it. I was, in a single moment, reminded of both God's perfect consistency and the magic of common occurrences. The ultimate fresh start.

I looked down at Caroline and smiled. Together, we marveled at the beautiful sunrise (the brilliant kind that happens only after a rainstorm) as it unfolded in front of us.

She made a shape with her fingers and thumb, like a duck opening and closing its beak, and pinched my hand. "Only the people who get up early get to see this. So we're the early birds," she said, "and this is our secret handshake."

I laughed then, but Caroline, Tyler (her twin brother), and I still do that same handshake now, months later.

That morning, God reminded me of His absolute certainty. He reminded me that when everything else in the world feels unsure and ever-changing that He is almighty, forever, and solid. He reminded me that sometimes a fresh start isn't found in a magnificent transformation, but in focusing our hearts on the signs, the slivers, the surprises and delights right in front of us. There is magic in the ordinary, if we dare to see it and create it.

The Lord's unfailing love and mercy still continue, fresh as the morning, as sure as the sunrise (Lamentations 3:22–23 GNT).

There are times in our lives when everything feels uncertain, even the ground we stand on. We have questions, worries, fears, concerns. The world seems as if it's moving so quickly and we have so much responsibility to keep up. We crave change, something big and quick to alleviate our pain, a fresh start. In those moments, in all moments, it's vital to remember that while this world may be ever-changing, God is not.

Over the next few months, I invite you to join me throughout my reflections, as we uncover the steadiness of the Lord and the richness of His love for us through big and small moments: in the comfort of a homemade chicken soup at the end of a cold day, in the joy of a little boy who finally lost his first tooth, and even in the sunrise after a storm.

Years ago, when I first created the Simplified Planner, I imagined you, with your cup of coffee or tea, a pen in hand, seated at your kitchen table, enjoying a few quiet moments before the kids awoke or before getting ready for work. I loved the idea that this tool would help you navigate your day and be your constant companion as you took care of whatever it was that mattered to you. And now, I'm honored to be with you during that quiet time in a new way.

Join me at the end of this book to explore the importance and nuance of a carefully crafted morning routine—one tailored to your needs and your season—to help you prepare your heart and mind for the day.

My prayer is that this morning devotional will come alongside you as you sit down to plan your day and fill your well, inspiring you to find delight in the ordinary, to create magic in your home, and to celebrate God's unchanging, unfailing love for us hour after hour.

Just don't forget to look out the window.

This is the start of the start of something new.

WEEK

01

It's a New Day

Every good and perfect gift is from above, coming down from the Father
of the heavenly lights, who does not change like shifting shadows.

JAMES 1:17 NIV

Hi, friends. It's a brand-new day. The start of something new. The past is behind us. The sun has risen. A new season is ahead. As you look out over the day or the year ahead, or even the next one hundred days we will journey together, what will you do with the time? Will you proactively plan it or will you allow it to happen to you as it may? Will you embrace change and growth, or is this a time to strengthen yourself for all that's ahead? At the end, how will you reflect on the time? Grateful for your steadfastness and adventurous spirit? Happy you rested when necessary and took care of yourself?

Spend some time today creating a bucket list for the next one hundred days. Consider the memories you'll be glad you made and the goals you'll be glad you reached, as you look back over this time. We never know what lies ahead, but we can know a few things for sure: (1) God's love and provision never change. They are sure and steady. (2) Each moment we have is a gift. Together, over the next one hundred days, let's use our time wisely and practice gratitude for God's mercies and delights.

What big or small memories do you hope to make this year? Do you have a goal to read one book every month? Or to strengthen your body? Or to go on a camping trip with your family? Today, write your bucket list for the next one hundred days and even the next year and put those plans on your calendar.

What Matters Most

*Commit your work to the L*ord*, and your plans will be established.*

PROVERBS 16:3

Every January, I love the practice of giving myself a focus for the next twelve months, a word of the year. This focus is one that will not change as the seasons change. It will not shift as the tides shift or as the events of the world unfold. Instead, it will remain my focus throughout everything the next twelve months brings my way.

In the past, I've embraced words like *wholeness, love, grace,* or *growth.* Your focus doesn't need to be complex but also shouldn't be too general. Instead, it should be one word that encompasses exactly what you hope to achieve, to reflect on, and to excel in during the coming months. Consider words like *simplicity, faith, servitude, consistency, strength,* and *resilience.* With each big and small decision you make, reflect on how each either supports or detracts from your focus. This simple thought process will bring awareness to your intentions and choices.

As James Clear said in his book *Atomic Habits,* "Every choice you make is a vote for the person you wish to become."[1] By measuring your decisions against your word of the year, you will actively build the life you wish to have.

> *Often, the deep desires of my heart are revealed to me through prayer. They even surprise me sometimes, and they come into my thoughts during my time with God. Begin by praying for guidance as you choose your focus. Then write your word of the year here: _____. How will you actively pursue this focus?*

An Intentional Edit

A time to seek, and a time to lose; a time to keep, and a time to cast away.

ECCLESIASTES 3:6

The beginning of a new year, new venture, or new season always inspires me to freshen up our home. I love making it feel thoughtful and welcoming, and I also find that decluttering our space helps us function better inside it. Simplifying across the board is a tall order, though. Several years ago I created The Simplicity Challenge and host it annually on social media. By breaking the process of simplifying and decluttering into bite-size tasks spread across a longer period of time, we're able to accomplish more and give our attention fully to each area.

Consider your kitchen today (perhaps the most frequented room in your house). What matters most to you about this space? Is it a gathering place for your big family after busy days? Do you love to cook and create delicious meals for yourself and others? Could simplifying this space actually honor your values, and support the things that are most important to you?

What could you do today in your kitchen that will simplify and infuse some joy into your morning routine? How might a simple coffee station help shape your morning? Could you set your favorite tea cup out for tomorrow? Joy can be found in the smallest of things.

 Do you have drawers or cabinets that are overflowing with objects in your kitchen? Using two trash bags (one for donations, one for trash), quickly go through each space in your kitchen. As you go, reflect on your goals for this space. Keep the best, favorite, and necessary and remove the rest. In time, your experiences in this space will be improved by your edit.

Joy in the Journey

This God—his way is perfect; the word of the LORD proves
true; he is a shield for all those who take refuge in him.

2 SAMUEL 22:31

I believe deeply that there is joy to be found in the mess of life. I'll never forget one afternoon when my toddler twins and five-year-old sat at the island in our kitchen, enjoying an early dinner of spaghetti. Their faces were covered in spaghetti sauce as they tried to get the noodles (which I'd cut up for easy eating) into their mouths. They were so happy. And all I could think was, *This place is a mess.* You know the feeling. Their joy is palpable and your anxiety is rising, thinking of all the cleaning you'll have to do. As my children got older and I began to actively press against my perfectionist tendencies, I felt something inside of me begin to loosen.

Granted, it's still there: my desire to live in a perfectly tidy home at all times (despite the fact that five humans, three of them small, live here). But it's less intense. God doesn't expect perfection from us. In fact, every single one of us falls short of perfection, of the glory of God. Order and tidiness are admirable and important goals, but what are we missing when we don't fully live our lives for fear of mess or disorder? There's so much joy to be found in the process of truly living—not just when life is cleaned up.

 Do you struggle with perfection? Who defined that standard for you? Social media? Your mother? Your neighbor who seems to always have it all together? Consider the perfect afternoon, the delight of a kid in a swimsuit with a water hose in a backyard, bare feet stomping through mud. The squeals, the laughter, the mess of it all. Sounds perfect, doesn't it?

Time to Check in with Yourself

The Lord your God is with you, the Mighty Warrior
who saves. He will take great delight in you.

ZEPHANIAH 3:17 NIV

I've created moments of pause throughout this book because I think it's vitally important for us to be still and reflect—to check in with ourselves, if you will. It's so easy to get caught up in the busyness of life. Being still does not come naturally to everyone. But it's in the stillness that we can know God. And so, you'll see that every week, we'll have some type of check-in time together.

Consider these check-ins like coffee with a friend. We've known each other forever and we've come to meet in a quaint, little café in your neighborhood. Sipping our coffee, I reach for your hand and ask, "How are you?" Maybe that question gives you pause. So often we respond to this question with "great" or "fine, thanks." But what I'd like you to do is stop and listen.

Listen to the rhythm of your heartbeat. Is it fast or is it slow? Place your hand on your stomach. Is it full or is it empty? Looking inward, how are you feeling? What are you learning? What are you seeking? What are you thirsty for? Now, look upward. Where is God leading you? What is He asking of you? In what ways do you feel aligned with God's will for your life right now, and in what ways do you feel like you may be pressing against it, hoping for a different outcome?

When I ask the words today—"How are you?"—pause, let yourself breathe, and reflect on how you really feel.

 Now that we are at the end of the first week, how can you realign with your intentions for this month? Offer your intentions to God through prayer today.

6

Reflection

We made it, friend. One week together, searching for God's mercy and delight, inviting Him to step into our mornings and guide our days. Use this page to reflect on the week and check in with yourself. Perhaps you have more ideas for your kitchen edit you'd like to jot down, or maybe you need simply to be still and reflect on God and share what's on your heart. I invite you to pause, reflect, and rest.

"See, the former things have taken place, and new things I declare; before they spring into being I announce them to you." Isaiah 42:9 NIV

WEEK

02

Just Do the Thing

Endurance produces character, and character produces hope.

ROMANS 5:4

Do you have a dream in your heart? A skill you'd like to learn or a goal you'd like to achieve? The kind that keeps getting pushed to the back burner in lieu of all the other responsibilities on your plate? Often, we tell ourselves we'll get to those things "when the time is right." When we have more time or money or when we lose more weight. But really, if you started today, in a month (or even a week!), you might be amazed at the progress you can make, starting as you are right now.

Tyler, the older of my twins, had just turned six when he attempted to ride a two-wheeled bike. He'd watched his twin sister ride circles around him for a few months but wasn't ready to risk falling down. One day, he put his helmet on and told me it was time. After a few falls, he threw his helmet and declared, "I'm a two-wheel quitter!" Stifling my giggles, I knelt to the ground, kissed his knees, and looked him squarely in the eyes. "You have to fall a few times, before you can really ride. It's part of it, buddy. You've got this." After a few more tries, he had it down pat! He zoomed past me and yelled, "Mom! I'm so happy about me!"

Are you ready to be "so happy about you" too? What have you been putting off for fear of failure? Isaiah 40:29 tells us of God's promise to strengthen us when we are weak: "He gives strength to the weary and increases the power of the weak" (NIV). Let us ask for strength today, then go out and do the thing.

God Meets Us Where We Are

I sought the LORD, and he answered me; he delivered me from all my fears.

PSALM 34:4 NIV

The Message version of this verse says, "GOD met me more than halfway, he freed me from my anxious fears." I love this verse so very much because there are times when we feel far away from God. We feel as if we've lost our way and we can't hear Him. I'm reminded that if we turn to Him, He will find us. In Luke, Jesus told the parable of the lost sheep:

> Suppose one of you has a hundred sheep and loses one of them. Doesn't he leave the ninety-nine in the open country and go after the lost sheep until he finds it? And when he finds it, he joyfully puts it on his shoulders and goes home. Then he calls his friends and neighbors together and says, "Rejoice with me; I have found my lost sheep." (15:4–6 NIV)

This parable illustrates God's relentless love for us—the way that He meets us where we are, the way He pursues us. Even when we feel like we can't find our way out of a dark spot or a tough situation, all we have to do is turn our eyes and hearts to Him. He will meet us more than halfway. He will carry us. Further, Dr. Larry Crabb once said, "God meets us where we are, not where we pretend to be."[1] What a beautiful reminder that He already knows where we are.

How are you right now? Really? I invite you to pray this prayer.

Lord, here I am. Find me and deliver me from my brokenness. Carry me on Your shoulders and keep me with You. In Jesus' name, amen.

Kindness Counts

Be kind and compassionate to one another, forgiving
each other, just as in Christ God forgave you.

EPHESIANS 4:32 NIV

The kindest people I know weren't born that way. They became that way through life experiences that, more often than not, were hard. They've been left out. They've been bullied. They've suffered tragedies and hardships. They know, firsthand, the importance of tenderness and empathy because they've received it. They've been on the receiving end of a homemade meal dropped on their doorsteps. They've had their coffees paid for by a stranger on a particularly hard day. They've melted into someone's open arms after receiving difficult news.

Kindness breeds trust. Trust breeds friendship. As you go about your day today, consider the kindness of friends, family, and even strangers, and give just a little bit more. A little bit of kindness goes a long way and says a lot about who you are inside and where you've been.

Take a moment today to send a text message to a friend you haven't spoken to in a while. Give your spouse an extra-long hug. What a chain reaction you may spark!

The Relentless Pursuit of Rest

There is a time for everything, and a season for
every activity under the heavens.

ECCLESIASTES 3:1 NIV

If I have learned anything about entrepreneurship and building and creating and business and work, it is this: we have to work, hustle, push, sweat, stay up late, sacrifice, and use all our grit. And then we *must* relentlessly pursue rest, fuel, nourishment, wisdom, and filling up.

If we live or build or work leaning only to one side of the equation, we will burn out and all our work (or rest) will be in vain. Much like riding a bike. Much like the pursuit of balance. Much like we read in Ecclesiastes: "There is a time for everything, and a season for every activity under the heavens: a time to be born and a time to die, a time to plant and a time to uproot" (Ecclesiastes 3:1–2 NIV).

Your seasons may be just minutes long. Or they may be days, or they may be years. But they must be counterbalanced to help you stay upright. Never lean too far left or right for too long.

Like many of you, I've recently gone through a season of pushing and working. The pandemic brought more work, more virtual learning, and more stress. But I'm starting to wonder if we may be transitioning into a new season sometime soon. And I'm curious . . . when it is time, what will your next season be?

 Are you on the cusp of a transition? A new season in your life? Where have you recently been and, more importantly, where are you going? What counterbalanced action is it time for you to take?

Seek What You Need

Take delight in the Lord, and he will give you the desires of your heart.

PSALM 37:4 NIV

What is it that you need today? Is it hope? A sense of peace? A reminder that you're not alone? Whatever it is, I invite you to lean into the feeling, and actively seek what your heart desires. Have you been under intense pressure to keep the wheels on the bus, to keep up with the day-to-day, maybe to nurture little ones and answer a thousand questions? Do you need rest?

Have you been wrestling with doubt or loneliness, longing for the light at the end of the tunnel or someone to reach out a hand and pull you onward? Do you need a friend?

So often, we put blinders on and trudge forward, allowing every day to feel a little like the movie *Groundhog Day*. It's okay to press Pause, to listen to your thoughts, to acknowledge how your heart is feeling and what it needs.

 In this week's reflection pages, we're going to take a few minutes to complete the following thoughts: "I feel . . ." and "I need . . ." Offer a prayer of thanks for the ten minutes you're able to breathe deeply while you're waiting in the car line. Offer a prayer of gratitude for the friend who visits for a cup of coffee. Delight yourself in the Lord's offerings, however big or small today.

Reflection

We've gone through another week together. How are you doing? Are your mornings feeling more grounded, your routines more settling? This week we're going to reflect specifically on rest, how we feel, and what we need. Use this space to journal on this week's themes of kindness and rest. What season are you currently in? And how can giving and receiving kindnesses change your days?

_____

_____

_____

_____

_____

_____

_____

_____

_____

_____

_____

_____

_____

Today, I feel:

_____

_____

_____

In recent weeks, my dominant feelings have been:

_____

_____

_____

Today, I really need:

_____

_____

_____

In the coming weeks, I think I'll need:

_____

_____

_____

Here's what I'm going to do today to help fulfill those needs:

_____

_____

_____

A PRAYER OF THANKS

God, thank You for meeting my needs and being with me right where I am. Today, I'm so thankful for:

Be where
your feet
are.

WEEK

03

Be Where Your Feet Are

*I will instruct you and teach you in the way you should
go; I will counsel you with my loving eye on you.*

PSALM 32:8 NIV

I spent a lot of years working very hard to keep up with my perfectionism: to have the perfect house, the perfect appearance, the perfect family, the perfect career. I wanted so badly to have it all together, as it seemed everyone else did. I chased and I pushed and I planned. I worried about the future and fretted over the past. Seldom were my feet and my brain in the same place.

Then one day, while visiting my parents' house, I lay in the grass. I'm not sure what possessed me to do such a thing, but I lay in their big backyard, breathing in the cool air, listening to my kids play around me. And it was like a veil was pulled off my eyes. My senses felt everything when I paused. The temperature, the sounds, the prickles of the blades of grass on the backs of my arms. It was beautiful.

Since that moment, I've vowed to "be where my feet are," to actively pull my thoughts back into the very moment I'm living. To rejoice and fully experience the gift of each moment. Because God will guide my steps, I need to just tune in to Him. Not only will He help discern my path, but He will do so while keeping a loving eye on me, right where I am.

 As you go about your day, when your mind begins to wander to yesterday's problems and tomorrow's concerns, bring your focus back to the present moment. Remind yourself to be where your feet are, to experience the gift of the moments God's given you.

Avoid Complainers

Whoever walks with the wise becomes wise, but
the companion of fools will suffer harm.

PROVERBS 13:20

A dear friend of ours is currently the commanding officer of the Naval Air Station Pensacola. He gave our son Brady some life advice in a card for his tenth birthday, which has stuck with me ever since: "Avoid complainers." It's a simple statement, but carries so much weight. I asked him about it a few days later. His father, he told me, gave him that simple advice when he dropped him off at boot camp when he began his military career. "Remember to avoid complainers."

As the old adage goes, we are the company we keep. We may not always realize it, but the thoughts and statements of others impact the way we think and behave. We can choose to surround ourselves with people who are positive, who encourage us to be our best selves, or we can choose to spend time with those who gossip and complain. Let us be intentional about the company we keep and about the type of company we, ourselves, are.

What type of company are you? Do you tend to be the complainer or the encourager? Goodness knows we all can fall into negativity at times. But could we, perhaps, be more intentional with our words and actions? Could we actively pursue positivity as we go about our days?

A Decluttered Mind

*Do not be anxious about anything, but in everything by prayer and
supplication with thanksgiving let your requests be made known to God.*

PHILIPPIANS 4:6

Decluttering allows us to pause, consider, and decide. By editing our belongings, we reflect on our spending habits, the values of our past, and the life we want to have in the future. This practice helps remove distractions so that we can focus on what matters to us. We can declutter our homes, our wardrobes, our calendars, and even our hearts.

When I'm feeling overwhelmed, I like to apply the principles of decluttering a junk drawer to decluttering my mind. First, empty the drawer. Then, carefully consider each item, deciding to either keep or discard it. When my responsibilities and thoughts begin to overcrowd my mind and heart, I take out a piece of paper (or a poster board for ample space) and a pen. I then freewrite all the thoughts that come to my mind (a judgment-free brain dump, if you will). Perhaps I'm worried about an upcoming doctor's appointment or I need to replace my air filters or I'm curious which stain remover would work best on my white pants. *All* the thoughts go onto the paper. Some items may be concerns that need to be prayed over. Some may be tasks that need to be addressed. Some are thoughts that simply need released. But now you have them all in front of you, to be handled in an appropriate way.

The active pursuit of your own inner peace is worthy of your time and attention.

*Lord, I lift up these worries. I ask for Your guidance and wisdom as I
complete these tasks and carry these concerns. Draw near to me so that
I may have inner peace, even when my responsibilities are many. Amen.*

Be Well

*Do you not know that your bodies are temples of the Holy Spirit, who
is in you, whom you have received from God? You are not your own;
you were bought at a price. Therefore honor God with your bodies.*

1 CORINTHIANS 6:19–20 NIV

One January, I decided to become a runner. I'd never run a 5K and only once
had I ever run a full mile without stopping, many years ago. And it was painful.
But I was determined, so I ran. At first, I ran to slip into the pair of jeans I'd
tucked in the back of my closet. But as I wore out my shoes, I noticed something else happening inside me. My *why* began to shift. Soaking my sore legs
in Epsom-salt baths at night, I'd reflect on the amount of time I was able to
keep running, without stopping, that day. At first it was three minutes, then
five, and eventually ten. I'll never forget the day I ran a full mile without even
considering slowing my steps.

It wasn't the short-term push to achieve better times or longer runs that
changed me; it was the lacing of the shoes. Every morning, when the kids left
for school, I'd put on my sneakers. It was the daily action of slipping my shoes
on my feet, knowing I was going to put one foot in front of the other today,
just like yesterday, just like I'd do tomorrow. Consistency changed me. I never
did slip back into those jeans. Instead I gave them away and bought the cutest
jeans that fit my newly strong body. And that was the trophy at the finish line.

 *What can you do, today, to honor your body? To strengthen, nourish,
and care for it?*

Breath of Life

Then the LORD God formed the man of dust from the ground and breathed into his nostrils the breath of life, and the man became a living creature.

GENESIS 2:7

Do you ever begin to pray and find your thoughts are wandering and your focus on "getting it right" is too complex? Do you wonder if you're doing it right? I recently learned of an ancient practice called *breath prayer*. The act of breathing is so simple, it allows us to draw near to God—who first breathed life into us—without overcomplicating the exercise. One common breath prayer is The Jesus Prayer: "Jesus Christ, Son of God, have mercy on me."[1] The Jesus Prayer is turned into a breath prayer by pairing a few words with the inhale and a few words with the exhale.

Give it a try. *Jesus Christ, Son of God . . . have mercy on me.*

Or try this from Psalm 46:10: *Be still, and know . . . that I am God.*

You can also create your own version, to pray whatever you need. A few words in, a few words out. Breath work has been proven to have biologically healing effects on the body.[2] By engaging in this simple practice, we align our thoughts with our bodies, take the pressure off our minds to "get it right," and are able to more fully experience the presence of God.

Take a few moments to practice a breath prayer. Choose from one of the examples mentioned above or create your own. As you go throughout your day and feel worries or stress begin to arise, give yourself a few seconds to engage in a silent breath prayer.

Reflection

Here's another breath prayer that has been meaningful to me: *When I am afraid . . . I put my trust in You.*

Feel free to take this page and jot down breath prayers that are meaningful and specific to you. Maybe they are something you pray when you are anxious or overwhelmed. Return to these prayers as you need them.

You don't have to stay the same.

WEEK

04

Decision Fatigue

"For where your treasure is, there your heart will be also."

MATTHEW 6:21

Part of my love for simplifying comes from my sensitivity to decision fatigue. I have a propensity to feel overwhelmed when my mental load is too heavy. I'm a deeply feeling, overthinking type of person. I care about everything, a lot, and because I care so much about getting it right with the things and the people I care about the most, I greatly desire to remove or turn the volume down on the other stuff—the distractions. This is true for my home, my calendar, and my heart. I'm constantly editing and purging to protect and defend my treasures: my relationship with God, my people, my work, my home. I believe this is holy work. In Matthew, Jesus said not to "lay up for yourselves treasures on earth, where moth and rust destroy and where thieves break in and steal, but lay up for yourselves treasures in heaven, where neither moth nor rust destroys and where thieves do not break in and steal" (6:19–20). Now why does this matter? Because we are human and not of infinite capacity. When we give space to something in our lives, it detracts from everything else, so it's crucial that we're giving space to the things that matter most.

The next time you feel decluttering or editing is a priority that doesn't deserve much of your time, remember "where your treasure is, there your heart will be also" (Matthew 6:21).

What is your treasure right now? Is it time spent working? Time spent with your kids? Or is it something else—an addiction, a problem, or a worry you can't shake? Naming our treasure, be it good or hard, brings it to light.

Making a House a Home

By wisdom a house is built, and by understanding it is established; by knowledge the rooms are filled with all precious and pleasant riches.

PROVERBS 24:3–4

I arrived home to my parents' house late in the afternoon one day after an arduous, eight-hour drive. Recently married, I loved our new home in Tampa, but it was just that: new. I had new friends, a new job, a new home, a new everything. But as I drove up and saw my parents in all their giddy glory waving from the driveway, I felt the comfort of home soothe my tired soul. Tears came to my eyes and I realized how much I'd missed this place where I was known—where my people knew me, my stories, and the way I took my coffee.

Entering the front door, bags in hand, I smelled lasagna in the oven. The table was set for three, my bed was turned down, and fresh towels were waiting for me in the bathroom. Oh, to be loved. To be welcomed into a space that is warm and safe. Home is where we are comforted, remembered, soothed, nourished, and reminded of who we are deep inside. Home is a sacred place. And the keeping of such homes . . . it is heavenly work. Just as God makes a place for us in heaven, it is so precious and valuable to make a place for one another here on earth.

Where do you feel most at home? What is it about that place that soothes your soul in such a way? Is it the scent? The people? The atmosphere? Consider today one thing you might be able to do to cultivate that feeling of home in your own house for yourself and your people.

Turndown Service

"If you are faithful in little things, you will be faithful in large ones."

LUKE 16:10 NLT

The other day I woke up feeling really worn out. I hadn't exercised in a few days, work was piling up, my attention was naturally being drawn to the news, to my kids' school, to my messy house. I started a workout and gave a halfway effort while I thought, *Maybe I need more protein, maybe I should clean my house, maybe I should take a day off . . .* Or maybe life was just tiring?

And then, I looked upstairs and started thinking about my kids. If I can't pinpoint the source of feeling worn out, how can they express how they're feeling? So I walked upstairs and I cleaned their rooms. Yep. I did the whole thing for each one of them. I turned down their beds. I turned on the dim "little lights" next to their beds. I put their favorite stuffed animals on their pillows.

If we feel overwhelmed sometimes, our children must definitely be feeling overwhelmed, only with fewer words and less understanding. If we can do anything at all to soften the difficulties of daily life, let us do it. What a beautiful way to spread love, to create delight. To love and serve unconditionally, just as God loves us. Whatever the day held for them, my little ones crawled into fresh sheets, their favorite stuffed animals nearby, in clean rooms, lit just right. It was a little thing, but I could tell it meant a lot.

What small, intangible way can you create delight or comfort for your family today? Is there something you could do for yourself today to bring an ounce more joy into the day-to-day?

Playtime

But Jesus said, "Let the little children come to me and do not hinder them, for to such belongs the kingdom of heaven."

MATTHEW 19:14

We can never underestimate the importance of play. My son Tyler is a LEGO-building machine. He can craft airplanes, castles, even dragons in the blink of an eye. His creativity truly knows no bounds. I've made it a point to get on the floor with him at least once a day to give him a few minutes of my undivided attention—a few moments when I'm not distracted by work or having a conversation while picking up the living room; these few moments are his alone. It may be only four or five minutes, but that time, spent on his level, meeting him exactly where he is, is priceless.

Four or five minutes wiping countertops or putting away all the shoes that gather by the front door may give me a clean house, but four or five minutes spent pouring into the cup of my little boy (in just the way he feels loved the most) means so much to him. I'd say that's a pretty good time swap.

 How can you swap just a few moments of your time today for someone you love? Or, alternatively, how can you devote a couple of minutes to filling your own well with a catnap, a warm bath, or a walk around the block? Don't underestimate the power of play in your own life! Feel the freedom to put a puzzle together, swing in the backyard, or play a board game.

You Don't Have to Stay the Same

"For I know the plans I have for you," declares the LORD, "plans to prosper you and not to harm you, plans to give you hope and a future."

JEREMIAH 29:11 NIV

Someone wrote to me on social media once, after I'd shared my heart about a current event I found meaningful, and told me to "stick to planners." It hurt. Not because she'd meant it in a malicious way, but because I realized I was being told to stay in a box. I realized there was someone in the world who, for her own comfort, would prefer if I stayed inside the box she'd mentally put me in: the planner girl.

What transpired from that message (which I didn't respond to), was actually a lot of growth for me. Who wants to be two-dimensional? Who wants to be told they have to stay the same forever and ever? Should I just stay "the planner girl" forever? Or was it okay for me to be the planner girl, the writing girl, the adventurous woman, the literature lover, the fierce mama bear, the maker of the best nachos this side of the Mississippi, and whatever else I grew into? Yes! Yes. And it's okay for you too. Never box yourself in. Never allow someone else to define your limits. And always remember, it's okay to grow and change, to evolve and become.

 Are you holding yourself back by staying inside your box? By staying inside the lanes someone else defined for you? Define the box you've created for yourself and spend a few minutes dreaming about who you might become if you begin to tiptoe outside of it.

Reflection

This week stretched me in some ways. It reminded me that decision fatigue is normal, but we can automate and simplify some things in our lives to give ourselves a little more margin—and that margin is crucial to creating a home, letting ourselves play, and allowing ourselves to grow.

Here are a few things to think about as we wrap up this week.

1. Do you have some regular (daily, weekly, monthly) tasks that bog you down? Can you automate any of them? Think of things like setting up automatic bill pay, delivery for prescriptions, or other tasks that could be done automatically or more efficiently. Write your list and then do *just one* of them today.

2. What makes your house feel like home? For you? For your people? Do you have a favorite homekeeping task that energizes you and comforts you?

_____

_____

_____

_____

_____

_____

_____

3. What's that one thing for you that really feels like play? That activity or hobby that makes you forget your worries and get lost in the moment. When was the last time you let yourself play? Even if you can't do that thing today, mark it on your planner, and make a plan to play.

_____

_____

_____

_____

_____

_____

_____

4. What habits or mindsets make you feel stuck? Have you labeled yourself as something—good or bad—that's inhibiting your growth and trapping you in a box? What would stepping out of that box look like for you?

_____

_____

_____

_____

_____

_____

_____

5. Take a breath. Check in with yourself and with God. Feel free to use this page for gratitude, prayer requests, or to-do lists.

_____

_____

_____

_____

_____

_____

_____

_____

God is unfolding a beautiful story in you.

WEEK

05

A Note to You

*Be kind to one another, tenderhearted, forgiving one
another, as God in Christ forgave you.*

EPHESIANS 4:32

Here's a letter I wrote to my daughter that perhaps you need to read too:

*Sweet one, you are a bright, shimmering sunshine just waiting to warm the world.
You bring delight wherever you go. And you feel all of life so very deeply. I see it
in your tears, in your prayers, in your eagerness to help others. You want to know
that you matter, that your place in this world is extremely important. I am writing
to tell you yes, yes it is. I love you; God loves you. When you are sad. When you are
mad. When you are confused and when you are angry. It's okay to feel things in
a big way. Those tears mean you are being moved, moved to action in some way.*

*When we aren't sure how to handle our emotions or big feelings, that's when God is
inviting us to seek Him out. To turn to Him and ask questions. To lay our thoughts
and worries at His feet. I invite you to do that too. God is unfolding a beautiful
story in you, and if you seek Him first, before your own understanding, He will fill
you with knowledge and guide your steps. Never turn down the volume on your
caring heart. Never let the world stamp out those big feelings. God made you with
an enormous heart on purpose.*

 *Do you ever criticize yourself for your tears? Or for getting your
feelings hurt? I invite you to look deeper into those emotions to see
God's truth in them. What is He teaching you about your hurts and
your worries right now? How might He be preparing you for the next
chapter of your story?*

Love Never Fails

Love never fails.
1 CORINTHIANS 13:8 NIV

The words above are inscribed inside my husband's wedding band. In the book of 1 Corinthians, these words follow the familiar passage: "Love is patient, love is kind. It does not envy, it does not boast, it is not proud. It does not dishonor others, it is not self-seeking, it is not easily angered, it keeps no record of wrongs. Love does not delight in evil but rejoices with the truth. It always protects, always trusts, always hopes, always perseveres" (13:4–7 NIV).

We don't always get it right. Like most couples, we have disagreements. We regrettably raise our voices from time to time. We don't always see eye to eye. I did some digging into this passage and realized that Paul wasn't actually referring to romantic love here. (Don't worry, we didn't take it off of his ring—it's still very applicable!) Paul was describing divine love: God's unfailing, unbreakable, unshakable love for us . . . even though we get it wrong sometimes, even though we may disagree with Him, even though sometimes we raise our voices at Him. First John 4:16 tells us God *is* love.

That, to me, paints a picture of a God who is so steadfast. It makes me consider how patient, kind, and giving God is. He knows our hearts, our sins, our secrets, and He loves us just the same. How lucky are we to have a Father who truly knows us and delights in us all the same.

Consider what it means to have a love that is unshakable. What brings strength to a love like that? What forms the frame that holds that kind of love up in a storm? I think we may find our answers in the words preceding "love never fails": patience, kindness, honor, truth.

In the Waiting

"Don't be afraid, for I am with you. Don't be discouraged,
for I am your God. I will strengthen you and help you. I
will hold you up with my victorious right hand."

ISAIAH 41:10 NLT

The messy middle is the hardest part. When the homework project is halfway done and the room is a mess. When the kitchen renovation is at peak craziness and you're cooking out of the back bedroom. When a loved one is in treatment, but not quite yet cured. When you're waiting for the results, and the anticipation feels as if it may drown you. When you're aching for that significant other, that baby, that job. When you're slowly adding one more day to your sobriety calendar and choosing yourself over the addiction minute after minute. When you're waiting, putting one foot in front of the other, hoping to get to the next day.

I once heard someone say, when you can't take one more step forward, move just an inch. And sometimes it doesn't even have to be a whole inch—just make sure you're not moving backward. Move forward any way you can. And, if you can't move forward, try stepping to the side. Some seasons, the strongest thing we can do is move sideways. When the grief, the struggle, the fear, or the yearning feels like it may do you in, move forward or move sideways. Seek first the kingdom of God and trust that He will be with you in the messy middle places.

How will you move forward or sideways today? Celebrate your progress, even if it is tiny. You are one step closer to who you are becoming.

When Things Aren't Working

Do not be conformed to this world, but be transformed by the
renewal of your mind, that by testing you may discern what is
the will of God, what is good and acceptable and perfect.

ROMANS 12:2

Do you ever feel like things just aren't working for you? Like the path you're on isn't the one you charted, planner in hand, pen flying, as you told yourself you'd wake up at 5:00 A.M., eat only healthy food, and swear off mindless Instagram scrolling forever? Do you ever stop and look behind you, wondering how in the world you ended up here, in this place that is so far from the perfect path you carefully plotted? I have.

Best-laid plans made under the guise of "major transformation" often die hard. And it takes a certain something to (a) realize you're far from where you wanted to be and (b) do something about it. So what do we do when we realize we've ended up somewhere we never intended to go? A major transformation would be nice (preferably the kind that doesn't require a lot of work), but more often than not, that's not the solution. Implementing small habits and good choices, little by little, is how true transformation happens. Every choice you make takes you either one step closer or one step farther to the path you want to be walking.

 What path are you on today, and who are you becoming? Are you proud of who she is, or is it time to implement some new habits and let go of others? Is there a small step you can take today to get back on the path?

Abundant Blessings

I praise you because I am fearfully and wonderfully made;
your works are wonderful, I know that full well.

PSALM 139:14 NIV

I sat on the edge of a beach chair in the dead of winter with my toes in the cold sand and tears pooling in my eyes. We desperately wanted a second baby. We'd been trying for years. My heart ached with longing for a little brother or sister for Brady. And yet, I felt immense guilt for wanting more than the blessing we'd already been given in him. I prayed God would help me find my way to a whole heart—be it through adoption, in vitro fertilization (IVF), a miracle, or even confidence that our family was, in fact, complete as a family of three.

A year later, on January 28, 2015, two tiny miracles conceived through IVF, who'd survived a tumultuous pregnancy, while I was put on weeks of bedrest and endured multiple hospital stays, were placed in my arms. Tyler and Caroline's birthday is a day I remember as being abundantly blessed. Not just by their birth but by God's steadfastness through my pain, the way He used that pain to create space for intense tenderness and empathy, and how I grew stronger through it all. If you are praying for your own wholeness, for your own answered prayers, I make space for you today. I hold you in my thoughts today, and every January 28. Sure as the sunrise, God is near, even in the midst of our pain.

 What prayer is sacred to you? What desire in your heart do you dare not speak because it's too precious, too fragile? I pray for that, for you today.

Reflection

The messy middle. Many parts of life are lived in the waiting, the trying, the failing, and the trying again and waiting some more. Sister, if you are in the messy middle, borrow this prayer:

Lord, You know the depths of my heart. You know me inside and out. You came before and You will go after me. Hear my tender prayers. Soothe my aching heart. Shape me as You will, while I wait.

Just like I would tell Caroline, I want you to remember that God is unfolding a beautiful story in you. You matter. And He is near. Share your heart with God.

you, my dear, are the asset.

WEEK

06

Prepare a Place for Love

We are his workmanship, created in Christ Jesus for good works,
which God prepared beforehand, that we should walk in them.

EPHESIANS 2:10

I've found that to be able to best love others completely and wholly, with the grace and patience and kindness Paul described in 1 Corinthians, I have to nurture and cultivate those traits in myself. Because when I am overwhelmed, I'm less likely to be patient. When I am overtired, I'm less likely to show grace. And when I am hurting or need healing, I'm less likely to be kind. Caring for ourselves makes us better poised to care for others.

I consider this idea as it relates to my children often. I love them with my entire heart. It's wild how your heart can grow to proportions you never thought possible, with each child brought into your family. I want to give them the very best of myself. But sometimes, after a long day, when my little ones come home from school and their backpacks explode all over my clean living room, and they begin arguing over the last bag of Goldfish, my grace, patience, and kindness tanks feel somewhat empty.

We can't always prepare for when our tanks will feel empty, but sometimes we can. We can stock the Goldfish basket in advance, for example. We can create a routine for unpacking backpacks and placing water bottles in the sink. And we can allow ourselves a couple of minutes alone in the bathroom to take a few deep breaths before we respond to our tiny, wonderful humans.

What can you prepare in advance to avoid your tanks getting empty? What pain points in your day sometimes make grace, patience, or kindness hard to come by? How can you alleviate those to better love your people?

46

Protect the Asset

Am I now trying to win the approval of human beings, or of God? Or am I trying to please people? If I were still trying to please people, I would not be a servant of Christ.

GALATIANS 1:10 NIV

One way we can show love to ourselves is found in 1 Corinthians: love "always protects, always trusts, always hopes, always perseveres" (13:7 NIV). To protect ourselves, we have to put boundaries into place—to protect our time, our energy, and our resources. Sometimes boundaries can be viewed negatively, but creating healthy boundaries is actually a wonderful way to take care of yourself. Boundaries allow us to perform, work, and love to the best of our abilities.

In Greg McKeown's book, *Essentialism*, he asserts that we must "protect the asset."[1] Well, you, my dear, are the asset in this equation. Is there a leak in your well? And how can you properly fix that leak to protect the asset? Is your calendar too full of commitments for you to spend time with God each morning? Consider scheduling your first work meetings a little bit later in the day. Is your mind too overwhelmed with the management of multiple children's schedules to be able to, with patience and love, read stories and tuck your kids into bed each night? Perhaps your spouse can take on sports practices and schedules. Is your phone constantly pinging and ringing during the day, distracting you from your work? Turn nonessential notifications off, protecting your brain space and focus during those vital hours.

How can you love yourself by setting some healthy boundaries today? What areas of your life could use a little more structure and definition?

DAY 28

He Sees You

*O LORD, you have searched me and known me! You know when I sit
down and when I rise up; you discern my thoughts from afar.*

PSALM 139:1–2

To the mother who wonders if anyone sees the work she does. The crumbs repeatedly swept from behind the table. The stains gently treated on the soccer jersey. The pillows neatly arranged every night before bed. The favorite coffee creamer repurchased. The sunscreen restocked. The school forms completed and tucked into backpacks.

Thank you.

The work you do matters. The rhythm of your role may feel redundant, but take heart. This is the holy work of living. The nurturing of the details. The behind-the-scenes magic that keeps wheels spinning, life moving, families flourishing. Though your tasks may feel mundane, these are an invitation to find God in the day-to-day. To seek Christ in our obedience to Him. Galatians 6:9 reminds us: "Let us not grow weary of doing good, for in due season we will reap, if we do not give up." Keep going.

Pray with me: "Lord, when the dishes pile up, when I question my relevance, when the to-do list runs off the page, remind me of who I am in You. Because I bear Your image, I matter. I pray that You'll remind me that love is a choice. May I choose love in every task."

Trophies

Nothing in all creation is hidden from God's sight.

HEBREWS 4:13 NIV

In the very top of our kitchen cabinets, there is a plastic gold trophy. It's Mickey Mouse, actually, and it looks like an Oscar. It is a running joke in my house that sometimes someone needs a trophy. It isn't joked about in a mean way; in fact, it's more of a loving, "I see you" sort of way. Sometimes Mom or Dad or one of the kids does something seemingly mundane but ultimately important. Another dinner made and served. A garage cleaned and organized. A difficult test passed. We like to bring the Mickey trophy out to say, "We know what you did, and we want to give you a pat on the back."

Our lives are full of tasks and work that don't often get recognized. I'd love a trophy for the laundry I folded this morning and the chicken soup I made last night, for instance. But I remind myself that while acknowledgment (and thank-yous) are nice, nothing is hidden from God. He knows and values the hours I spent sewing costumes for the school play. He sees the monotonous meal planning and dish washing. He even saw the time I spent going through my kids' shoes to wash the dirty ones and donate the outgrown ones.

Everything you do is seen. While it may not always be rewarded with a trophy, the work you do matters.

 How can you recognize someone in your life for their service, their work, or their small, good choices made in love today? Choose one person in your life and send them a message to let them know you see what they do, and that you're grateful.

Reflection Time

This is the day that the LORD has made; let us rejoice and be glad in it.

PSALM 118:24

Let's stop and savor the goodness and growth we've experienced during these last thirty days. A cup of tea shared with a friend near the fire. An evening dinner table scattered with crumpled napkins, wine glasses, plates with crumbs, pie dishes half full. A thoughtful plan made for the year at work. A peaceful winter wonderland scene, snow kissing the branches of every tree and limb in sight. Progress toward new goals, or perhaps reworked goals that feel more like simple habits going well.

As you know by now, I love the practice of reflecting on time gone by as we look ahead to the next season to come. Consider for a few minutes the blessings God's given you the last month. How has He worked in your life? What's one thing you've learned? One problem you've overcome, one person you've forgiven, or one way you've forgiven yourself?

 Use this time to reflect and set your intentions for the month to come.

Reflection

It's so easy to forget to love ourselves, to protect the asset—and remember that *we* are the asset—and to remember that our work matters.

This week, let's reflect on the delights God has brought to us, the kindnesses He has shown us, and some ways that we can show kindness to ourselves. God loves you so. Be kind to you.

What kind things have others done for you that have made you feel seen and loved?

_____

_____

_____

_____

_____

_____

What kind things could you do for yourself in the coming days?

_____

_____

_____

_____

_____

What moments of delight did God bring your way this month?

_____

_____

_____

_____

_____

_____

_____

_____

How have God's mercies unfolded in your life the last few weeks?

_____

_____

_____

_____

_____

_____

_____

_____

What are your intentions for the next thirty days?

_____

_____

_____

_____

_____

_____

How would you like to grow, spiritually, in the next month? What can you do, tactically, throughout your days to help get you there?

_____

_____

_____

_____

_____

_____

Lord, thank You for this last month. Thank You for the moments You've brought warmth to my life during this winter season: for _____ and _____. I pray You will guide my decisions and choices during the coming days as I focus on _____.

Love
one
Another

WEEK

07

DAY 31

Table for Two

*Therefore encourage one another and build one
another up, just as you are doing.*
1 THESSALONIANS 5:11

A few years ago, I was on the tail end of a long book tour. I'd visited many cities, meeting new friends and promoting my recent book. It was so much fun, but I was tired and my heart was weary. I had a few stops left to go before returning to my family. My friend and coworker whom I'd been traveling with, Hannah, arranged for us to have breakfast at a beautiful restaurant in downtown Nashville before that day's event.

I walked in and let the hostess know we needed a table for two. The restaurant was packed, so I kept close to her, weaving in and out of people. "Here you go," she said, pointing to a table . . . full of people. "Oh, I'm sorry, it's just the two of us . . ." I started to say. Immediately my head swung back to the table. There sat my entire team from work, some of my closest friends, who live all across the country (minus one who'd just had a baby), mouths covered, tears in their eyes, enormous smiles on their faces. I was floored. I'm not easy to surprise. I cried. We all cried. We work remotely and had only once been in the same room before! I couldn't believe all they'd done to get there.

How lucky we are to do life with others, to have friends who lift us up, who cheer us on, and who will fly across the country for books and breakfast.

 Who is your closest friend (or friends)? Send a quick text message to them today to remind them how much you care for them. To love and be loved is the greatest gift.

Rest and Refreshment

"I will refresh the weary and satisfy the faint."

JEREMIAH 31:25 NIV

After the event in Nashville, we went to the home of one of our teammate's in-laws. I'd been staying in hotels for more than a week and was looking forward to staying in a home. The family was on vacation, and we had the entire house to ourselves. I walked into the bedroom prepared for me and found that the sheets were neatly pressed and the pillows were fluffed just right. There was a phone charger on the nightstand and fresh towels in the bathroom. I could have cried, again. The care with which this home was prepared for us moved me in such a way that I try to prepare my home this way for guests now.

That night, we opened a bottle of red wine and sat together around the fireplace talking about the day's events and the epic surprise. I slept so soundly and awoke feeling refreshed and grateful. Bags packed, ready to head to the airport for my next stop, I made my way into the kitchen. There, on the counter, was a coffee maker, individual coffee pods of every flavor, sugar and stirrers, and to-go coffee cups with lids. There is no better medicine for a weary, tired traveler than a welcoming home, a place to rest her head—and of course, all the coffee she needs.

If you have a guest visiting soon, consider how you might prepare for them. If not, how can you care for yourself in such a way? What might you need tomorrow morning? Program the coffeepot to run before you wake. Lay out your clothes for the day. Pick up the living room so that you can wake to a tidy space.

Agape Love

He heals the brokenhearted and binds up their wounds.

PSALM 147:3

When I was in college, I got engaged to my long-term boyfriend. All my experiences with love circled around him. When we ended our engagement, I remember feeling so very alone, so unsure of who I was without him. Cue all the ballads playing from my CD player and all the tears. A friend invited me to church with her one Sunday evening and, since I had nothing better to do, I went with her. I'd been raised a Christian, but hadn't attended church a whole lot. That night, though, the ache in my heart unexpectedly cracked wide open.

That evening, my friend's pastor reflected on a kind of love I'd never considered before. An all-encompassing, fully forgiven, unconditional love. A love that could not be shaken. A love that will never leave. A love that won't change its mind, or fancy someone new, or let us down. That night, I learned about agape love. And after the closing prayer, I found myself on my knees, at the altar, praying for God to heal my broken heart. To sum up a long story, He did just that. But more than healing my heart, He drew near to me. His love and His Word were a soothing balm.

Have you experienced a broken heart? How did God meet you during that time? It's often when God cracks us wide open that we make space for Him the most.

Even Though

"My command is this: Love each other as I have loved you."

JOHN 15:12 NIV

I've found a little bit of magic in the "even though" part of God's love. God loves us completely *even though* we are sinners. God loves us totally *even though* we make bad choices sometimes. God loves us without ceasing *even though* we make mistakes. This verse is calling us to love like God loves. *Even though* we don't always get a thank-you. *Even though* we sometimes feel unappreciated. *Even though* those we love sometimes get it wrong.

Recently I had a friend who didn't feel loved or appreciated by her husband for all the work she did to keep the house tidy, to manage children's doctors' appointments and ballet lessons, and to prepare nutritious meals every day. She studied this verse at great length: *"My command is this: Love each other as I have loved you"* and decided to actively love her husband *even though*. When he had a long day, she made his favorite roasted chicken and potatoes *even though* he might not have thanked her. When she knew his dry cleaning was piling up, she took care of it *even though* he didn't acknowledge her kindness. When she found his shoes lying around the house, she'd graciously put them away for him *even though* she didn't really want to.

A tide changed in her marriage. He stopped to bring her flowers one afternoon. He brought home pizza early for dinner on a random Friday to give her a break. He even started picking up his shoes to help around the house more. Love begets love.

How can you love someone today, even though they may not reciprocate immediately?

"Thinking of You" Bags

"Whoever can be trusted with very little can also be trusted with much, and whoever is dishonest with very little will also be dishonest with much."

LUKE 16:10 NIV

When Brady was young, I traveled semi-often for work. I was a mother to a growing toddler and a growing business. This wasn't easy for either of us. So to soothe our sadness, I started making "thinking of you" bags for Brady to open while I was gone. They were numbered "day one," "day two," and so forth. Inside he'd find a toy car, a travel-size bubble bath, or a bouncy ball—something small to bring a little delight to his heart. I'd tuck notes inside, too, to be read by his daddy. Every night that we could, we'd FaceTime while he opened his "thinking of you" bag.

The toys were tiny and literally meaningless, but the routine of seeing each other's faces, knowing that smiles would be shared, was methodical, structured, and grounding for both of us. It rooted our days and reminded both of us what mattered most: that Mommy was off doing good work and that Brady was loved and treasured. Sometimes, when life is hectic, implementing a new routine or rhythm helps the dust settle and brings us back to what's most important. Maybe for you, it's not a surprise bag for a child. Instead, maybe it's making your bed every morning during a busy season, maybe it's five minutes of prayer at the end of every day, or maybe it's simply pausing to breathe when your worries begin to rise.

God has trusted you with both big and small things. How will you steward these? In the busyness of your life, what rhythm can you add to ground yourself to what's most important?

Reflection

Love is such a cherished gift, and yet sometimes it's easy to forget just how much the small things matter. I think sometimes it's the regular filling of cups—the daily acts of love—that can lead us to the bigger, grander moments of delight.

How can you love the people in your life today? This week?

_____

_____

_____

_____

_____

Is there a relationship in your life or a space in your heart that is feeling rather empty? Is there someone you can share this with in a meaningful way that could help you feel loved too?

_____

_____

_____

_____

_____

What God has
called us to,
God will walk
us through.

WEEK

08

Go and Do

"Peace I leave with you; my peace I give to you. Not as the world gives do I give to you. Let not your hearts be troubled, neither let them be afraid."

JOHN 14:27

Sometimes, as a writer, I worry that my skill will just leave me. That today will be the day that I sit down to put pen to paper (or fingers to keys) and I will have lost the ability to put words together in ways that help others feel seen, in ways that unlock some part of myself—and, at its best, ways that make any sense at all. I scurry around the room, cleaning my glasses, pouring one more glass of water, adjusting the temperature just so. Everything has to be right for that magic to happen.

But it's not true. What God has called us to, God will walk us through. That is certain. That doesn't mean our jobs will always be easy—whether we are writers, baristas, teachers, mothers, or doctors. Sometimes, the way we invite the very best of ourselves—of our hearts and our work—forward, is to simply do. Put one foot in front of the other. We choose to open the laptop, to wipe the jelly-covered mouth again, to make yet another latte for a customer. Some days it all flows out of us, and others, it's a struggle to even show up. But when we do, God meets us there. He shows up, too, and helps us keep going.

 When we do good work, in love, we honor the Lord. Ask God to walk alongside you today, as you go about your work.

Trust the Process

For by him all things were created, in heaven and on earth,
visible and invisible, whether thrones or dominions or rulers or
authorities—all things were created through him and for him.

COLOSSIANS 1:16

When writer's block hits me, I will find a closet to organize. I'll declutter and clean and get out my label maker. I will make the very best labels. I'll sort things by color, making sure the hangers are evenly spaced. I will control that closet until it is perfect. And by perfect, I mean *perfect*. My inner control freak does *not* like writer's block.

I will sit down with my laptop charged, my blank document pulled up on the screen, my favorite mug full of hot coffee by my side. Fingers poised above keys . . . and nothing. And so I find something I can control.

Ultimately, I'm learning over and over again that God is in control of everything, and that sometimes the best way forward is to take a detour for a little while, reset ourselves, and recognize that God wants us to trust that the process is in His care.

 Do you struggle with the messiness of the creative process or the tasks that fill your day? Whether cooking a meal or painting a masterpiece, pray for patience and trust in the process, and the growth that happens between beginning and end.

Your Seat at the Table

I sought the Lord, and he answered me and delivered me from all my fears.
Those who look to him are radiant, and their faces shall never be ashamed.

PSALM 34:4–5

Writing a devotional is something I've always wanted to do, and something I've been very, very scared to do. I was raised in a Christian, faithful family, but we weren't part of a church. I don't have stories of church camps and Sunday school, but I do have stories of dinners shared around a table, grace said by little ones with bowed heads, a meal lovingly prepared by a father and mother carefully stewarding their family in the ways of the Lord. Still, I don't write like many Christian writers. I'm not skilled in theological study. My faith is blossoming, still unfolding.

Recently I've learned about liturgy. And how liturgy, at its most basic definition, is the exchange of prayers, praise, and graces between God and His people. It's simple. It's rhythmic. It can be decidedly uncomplicated; it can connect to God and ground us in our faith. Wherever you are in your faith journey, God delights in you. Remove the shrouds of judgment, regret, and shame from where you are—whether you're a seasoned Christian returning to Him or simply curious about who Jesus is and what He came here for. I'm glad you're here with me.

Sometimes it's important to remind ourselves and others that we belong at the table. A seat was made and prepared for us, even before we chose to sit here. When we judge, regret, and feel shame over where we are in our faith journey, it only holds us back. Today, acknowledge where you are, embrace where you've been, and set your eyes— prayerfully—on where you're going.

On Bugs and Windshields

"Have I not commanded you? Be strong and courageous. Do not be frightened, and do not be dismayed, for the Lord your God is with you wherever you go."

JOSHUA 1:9

The truth about writing is that some days my fingers are on fire. My heart is burning with every word. Sentences get strung together in such beautiful and nuanced ways that I think God is pounding on my keyboard with me. On those days, I close my laptop, thank God for allowing me to live my dream, for developing this passion inside me that I feel born to do.

Other days, I question my life choices. I stare out the window and ponder on what I should make for dinner, the fact that my pants feel too tight, and whether or not they're still holding my prescription at the pharmacy. I'm convinced I have a terminal illness. Elbow cancer, to be exact. I write completely inept words that make zero sense when put together, and think perhaps my six-year-old could do a better job than I could. All is lost. I am terrible.

Some days we're flying on eagles' wings living out our life's purpose, and other days feel like life and our inadequacies are punching us in the face. That's okay. The trick to living life authentically, fully present, is to know that some days we're the bug and some days we're the windshield.

Is today your day? Or not? Embrace whatever it is. Take a break, do something different, or fill up that coffee cup and keep going. Do what you need to do when you don't feel inspired, then get back to work. The people who achieve things are the ones who keep going.

A Record for Reflection

Let this be recorded for a generation to come, so that a
people yet to be created may praise the LORD.

PSALM 102:18

A few years go, I opened my Bible from college. The pages of 1 Corinthians were dog-eared, underlined, highlighted. Words decorated the margins in different-colored ink. Reflecting on twentysomething-year-old Emily's journaling reminded me of who I was back then. And how I'd grown since then.

The practice of journaling is a beautiful one. Sometimes, it's even a form of prayer for me. I will jot down my thoughts, scrambled as they may be, and pour out my heart to the Lord on paper. I know God knows these thoughts as they move from my heart, to my head, to my hand. The exercise of reflection is so very eye-opening to me and I love to look back over old writings. So much is revealed through words I put on paper but may never say aloud.

Do you have a journal? If so, how has it helped you? And have you looked back on journals from years past? Can you see how you are growing?

Reflection

Whether you've been a lifelong journal writer or you've never put pen to paper, consider spending just a few minutes journaling as you begin your day. You can jot things down here, get a separate notebook or journal, or even record some thoughts in your planner. If you like the idea of freewriting but aren't sure where to start, here are a few ideas:

- A prayer journal where you record your requests, praises, and thanks to God
- A gratitude list to help focus on your blessings
- A narrative of stories and memories of your life
- A bucket list of your dreams and ideas
- Whatever you want it to be—no rules, just writing

Writing is a big part of my life. You may not feel the same way, but I think spending a few minutes a day jotting down our thoughts can be such a beautiful way of processing our experiences. The time it takes to write letters, words, and sentences gives our minds time to fully flesh out our worries, desires, and feelings.

To start, write your own prayer for today here:

God, thank You for _____.

Please give me a spirit of _____ .

I pray for _____ . Amen.

In this week's entries I shared some of the personal struggles with my work and my faith. What is God calling you to in this season, and how do you need Him to help you?

_____

_____

_____

_____

_____

_____

_____

As you've journeyed in your faith walk, what obstacles have you overcome? What struggles do you still need God's help to overcome?

_____

_____

_____

_____

_____

_____

_____

_____

_____

_____

Sometimes when we're in a dry or uphill season of life—be it in our faith, our relationships, or our work—we can feel distant from God. It's a bit too easy to forget that He's still right there beside us, going ahead of us, preparing a way for us.

Something that helps me during these seasons is to reflect on the ways God has shown up for me in the past. Even just the memories of those moments can lift my spirits and remind me that He is with me and for me.

Write down every memory you have of God showing up for you. Some examples for me are: God showed up for me when I begged Him for patience during a frustrating parenting moment last night. God showed up for me when I asked Him for courage to step out on stage and deliver my speech. God showed up for me when I prayed for strength to face a difficult doctor's appointment. He came alongside me each time.

Let's leave legacies of relentless Love.

WEEK

09

Two Ears, One Mouth

"He who has ears to hear, let him hear."

MATTHEW 11:15

My dad gives great pieces of advice. We like to say he's a walking billboard, quick with the inspirational one-liners. As a child, I loved to stand between him and the television while showing off my latest dance moves from ballet or telling him a story from the day or just being an oblivious kid. "Emily, you'd make a great door, but never a window," he'd tell me, implying that I was not, in fact, transparent. He also told me—because I was a precocious thing who *loved* to verbally unpack the day and had a commentary on absolutely everything— "Emily, remember, God gave you two ears and one mouth so that you can listen more than you talk."

As a parent now, I consider this second piece of advice often. When my children come to me with a problem or a situation that happened at school, I find myself hurrying the story along by asking multiple questions about the who, what, and where details. Following my dad's advice, though, I've found that if I instead allow the story to unfold, or the silence between thoughts to linger, space is made between us that draws more detail from my child. It's as if my careful listening invites them to pour out their hearts much more than my specific prodding.

At some point today, as you interact with another, pause while you actively listen. You may learn something wonderful and connect in a way you would have otherwise missed.

What is the best piece of life advice you've ever been given? How has it remained a part of your life over the years?

DAY 42

Safe Spaces

*Blessed be the God . . . who comforts us in all our affliction, so that
we may be able to comfort those who are in any affliction.*

2 CORINTHIANS 1:3–4

I have very vivid memories of lying on a plastic, green nap mat underneath my mother's wooden desk in her elementary school classroom. When I wasn't feeling well, my teacher would send me to my mom, who'd make sure I was generally okay (no fever or anything), then let me rest under her desk. It was my spot, and I felt so cared for there.

Looking back, I realize two things about these memories. First, my mom always held space for me. She was, and is, my safe place and my safe-place maker. As a child, this meant being wrapped in love and conversation at a dinner table, welcomed home to a warm bath after dance practice, and even tucked under her desk at school.

Second, she was a working mom who probably ached that she couldn't immediately take her daughter home. Worst case, she would call my dad to leave his office to fetch me or she'd call in a substitute so she could leave. But on these middle-ground days when I had a simple headache or an upset tummy, she'd make do. She had responsibilities and did the very best she could with what she had. And so, she arranged a little green nap mat under her desk. I'd lie there and listen to her teach, hearing her read stories to her students. Every now and then, she'd peek under the desk to check on me and smile.

 Motherhood is complicated. It's the most difficult job I've ever loved with my whole heart. I'm grateful for my mom's example. Who is the creator of safe spaces in your life? Where is your safe space now?

A Collection of Nails

One generation shall commend your works to another,
and shall declare your mighty acts.

PSALM 145:4

When I was a little girl, I collected cows. Not real cows, mind you. Little cow figurines, stuffed animals, and the like. At another point, I collected Troll Dolls, then Anne Geddes's precious portraits of babies, and later, ginger jars.

My grandfather, a construction superintendent, collected nails. Back in the 1960s, while overseeing the building of schools and commercial buildings, he went through a lot of nails. When a job was done, he'd inevitably have a handful turn up in the floorboard of his truck or in a corner of the warehouse. Back at home, he had a row of red Folgers coffee cans. On the side of each was a strip of duct tape where he'd written, in black marker, the names of each type of nail. He'd carefully sort his handful of nails into each container, to be used for his woodworking projects.

Before he passed away a few years ago, he gave those cans to my dad, his brothers, and to my brother. Along with his nails, he passed on his love for excellence in woodworking, for quality craftsmanship, and for diligent hard work. Each time I see those cans of nails, I'm reminded of his legacy of meticulousness, honor, and love. These treasures often make me think of my own legacy—what I will pass on to my children and grandchildren, perhaps not physically but emotionally and spiritually. Every big and small choice we make today shapes that eventual legacy. I hope mine will be one of relentless love.

 Imagine your loved ones remembering you in the future. What three words best describe the legacy you'd like to leave with the world?

On Precision and Mastery

Whatever your hand finds to do, do it with your might, for there is no work or thought or knowledge or wisdom in Sheol, to which you are going.

ECCLESIASTES 9:10

My family is a family of builders. No one will outwork a Cowan (my maiden name). We're like bumblebees. We have a hard time staying still and love to create and toil and fix and make. My mom makes meals and memories. My dad makes furniture and repairs. My brother makes new recipes and loves wood-working. I make books and craft words together. Our love for working hard and making things comes from a long line of builders, farmers, teachers, and homemakers.

Along with my grandfather's nails, my dad also inherited some tools. (My mom is none too pleased with this enormous collection of old tools in her garage, but it is very special nonetheless). Some are aged and rusted now, but they were used by the worn hands of men who valued precision and mastery (and wouldn't let you get away with cutting corners). My dad recently told me that he feels the presence of his father and grandfather when he's using those hand tools, some of his most prized possessions. As he works with these tools, he remembers their dedication to excellence, and all the lessons of craftsmanship they taught him. "Now," he said, "when I use their tools, I feel as though they're helping me finish something for the future."

Maybe this is why I still use my grandmother's KitchenAid hand mixer to bake cupcakes. Because it reminds me of making them with her.

 What values did your family instill in you? What values are important to you to pass on to others?

Frogs and Finality

*"So also you have sorrow now, but I will see you again, and your
hearts will rejoice, and no one will take your joy from you."*

JOHN 16:22

When I was a child, I had a pet frog named Jo Jo. I found him at a pet store up the street, and I vowed to love, protect, and care for him all by myself. I watched him swim and sometimes even talked to him while I got ready for school. He was a great pet for many years—a quiet little buddy that swam his laps and hung out with me in my room.

One day, I noticed Jo Jo's legs beginning to turn pink. Since Google wasn't yet a thing, I called the pet store where I'd purchased him. They informed me that Jo Jo may have what's called red-leg disease and that if so, he was dying. I know, I know—it was a frog. But I was devastated.

This was my first experience with the circle of life, the loss of someone (or something) I loved. The memory is so tender and yet also makes me giggle at my innocence. Upon hearing the news, I held vigil for my buddy during his last days. I stayed next to his tank until he took his last underwater breath. As my dad helped me bury Jo Jo in the side yard, I remember feeling like this very small loss was a very big deal. I had never felt the grief we're left with when someone (or something) we love passes away.

*No matter how big or small, the loss of someone (or something) we
love brings grief. May we remember that the sadness we feel is born
from the love we also feel. Two special feelings worthy of holding and
honoring.*

Reflection

This week I shared some memories of my childhood and my loved ones who shaped it. I don't take for granted what a gift it is to be raised by people who loved and supported me. Think back on your childhood—was it a gift or a burden? How has it impacted who you are today?

_____

_____

_____

_____

_____

Thinking on our legacies can be daunting—somehow a little scary and sad but also beautiful and purposeful. What kind of legacies have been left for you? What kind do you want to leave?

_____

_____

_____

_____

_____

_____

Breathe in the possibilities. Embrace the delights.

WEEK

10

Grace upon Grace

The steadfast love of the LORD never ceases; his mercies never come to an end; they are new every morning; great is your faithfulness.

LAMENTATIONS 3:22–23

Infertility is a journey that changed my life, but still a journey I would have never chosen. Bryan and I thought, once we were ready to have a child, we'd be blessed with one. But our path to grow our family looked much different than that. It was riddled with bumps, potholes, and more U-turns than I care to remember. Shots, appointments, procedures, medications, and an intense focus on a calendar filled our days for years. There were surgeries, measurements, tests, and so many disappointments. One pink line, every single month.

All of this work eventually brought me to my knees. I ached for a baby in a way I'd never ached for anything. I was a hard worker who believed I could outwork anything. Even this. I prayed to God for the strength to keep going, to better organize my medications, to be more on top of my strict diet, and to be able to rebound from disappointment. But instead, God invited me to stop.

And so we did. We paused, with our doctor's blessing. We put the medications out of sight. I ate what felt good to my body. We enjoyed just being husband and wife. Sometimes grace looks like finally reaching the goal, finally conceiving your long prayed-for baby. Sometimes grace looks like pumping the breaks, taking a nap, eating a cheeseburger, and loosening your grip on the wheel a bit.

God did a lot of work in my heart during our years of infertility. What seasons has God walked through with you? What did you learn during those times? What did His grace look like for you?

In-Between Moments

Rejoice in hope, be patient in tribulation, be constant in prayer.

ROMANS 12:12

There are a few moments in life that are so fleeting, they'll race right by us if we aren't paying close enough attention to grab onto them. Mine include, but are not limited to, the few minutes between Bryan's proposal and me picking up the phone to call my parents to share the news. For those few minutes, I cried. We dreamed. We stared at the ring together, at my hand with its new appearance, this symbol of forever slipped onto my finger. It was sheer bliss.

Another moment like this began with a craving for Twizzlers. I'd just quit my full-time job to pursue my entrepreneurial dreams and was fighting traffic on the long drive home. But Twizzlers. And so I pulled into our neighborhood CVS. I bought the Twizzlers and a pregnancy test. Probably the zillionth one I'd purchased that year. I went home, took the test, and threw it away. Negative. Moving on. But wait . . . digging it out of the trash, I saw the faintest appearance of a second line. No. Surely, no. It'd never happened before. And after a few minutes, there it was. Two solid pink lines. Our season of rest, the loosening of my grip on the wheel—it'd worked.

I remember looking out our bathroom window and seeing Bryan pull up. *He doesn't know,* I thought. *I know, and he doesn't know. This is the only moment in our lives I will hold this information to myself.* I said a prayer and ran to tell him the news.

 Reflect on your favorite moments of sheer, sacred joy. Maybe they are the big moments themselves? Or maybe they were the in-between moments like mine?

Mercy and Delight

You are altogether beautiful, my darling; there is no flaw in you.

SONG OF SOLOMON 4:7 NIV

There's something about writing that makes you live life with your eyes wide open. I've learned, though, that this is a lovely thing to practice. Moments of mercy and delight are all around us, but like our fleeting moments of in-between bliss, they will evaporate like snowflakes landing on warm palms if we don't pause long enough to notice them.

A butterfly flying in an open window. Fluttering in, then right back out. Little butterflies don't belong in houses; what could he be doing here? This is what hope feels like.

A genuine moment with a child, eyes locked. "Mommy, you're the very best." Please stay this age forever, my darling. This is what love feels like.

Rainy Saturday mornings, the kids watching cartoons outside our door, me curled up with you. You always said that spot was mine. I think I'll stay here a while, the rain reminding us of the warmth and safety of home, everything we love inside these walls. This is what trust feels like.

A North Carolina waterfall, hundreds of miles from home, the three of us totally outside of our comfort zones, relishing the mountain air, the adventure of the day, God's glorious creations on grand display, nature beaming at us from every direction. This is what growth feels like.

 Consider your moments of mercy and delight. God reveals Himself to us in these tiny moments, those fluttering lashes, the sound of the rain on our windows. As you move about your day, take note. Live today with eyes wide open.

84

Ordinary Mornings, Extraordinary Grace

From his fullness we have all received, grace upon grace.

JOHN 1:16

Today, take note of what brings you gladness. That which gives you pause or causes you to take a deep breath. These are glimpses of God's goodness in our lives, brought to life through moments and things, memories and sounds. Realizations and hope. In its biggest forms: a moment you wish you could freeze in time, and in its smallest: a sliver of grace, otherwise overlooked.

I wake up to the smell of fresh laundry, sheets cool against my skin. One eye open, I peek down at the floor next to me, and there you are in your pink sleeping bag, wearing your cheerleading camp T-shirt.

I stare at you a while, smiling at who you once were, all bright pink lips and big, bold, spunky laugh. And who you are now: deeply loving, a servant's heart, a laugh still the color of sunshine.

You wake, voice full of sleep, and say, "Hi, Mama. I'll make you some coffee, okay?" and you're off, wide awake in just a few seconds flat.

And now here I am, cup of coffee in my favorite Ted Lasso mug, brought to me by my favorite six-year-old barista who just learned how to work the Keurig. Splash of cream, made with love. Ordinary morning, extraordinary grace.

 Name your delights today. What's your ordinary moment full of extraordinary grace?

Breathe in the Possibilities

For God, who said, "Let light shine out of darkness," has shone in our hearts to give the light of the knowledge of the glory of God in the face of Jesus Christ.

2 CORINTHIANS 4:6

I invite you to step outside with me today. If you can, put on your slippers and take this book outside. Spend some time outside, in the middle of God's creation, while you consider all your current season has held. Together, let's breathe in the possibilities of a new day, a new season on the horizon, and breathe out some of the things we may need to release.

Are you up in time for the sunrise? If not, that's okay. But if you have a moment and a spot to see the outside world wake up around you, take in the sun and the sky. The clouds and the birds. The breeze on your face.

When we turn down the noise, the lights, and the distractions, we can see the magnificence around us in greater clarity. Perhaps it's a vibrant sunrise we're looking for. Or the joy in the mess at home. The delight in the difficulties at work. The new buds on the trees. Or the goodness in the people around us.

 Today, as we wrap up our first fifty days together, still yourself just for a moment, to take note of all the wonder around you. It is there, if only we pause long enough to see it.

Reflection

Life is full of ordinary moments and extraordinary graces. I shared a few during this week's readings, and I think these moments and gifts can range from the miraculous to the silly and sweet stuff of life that fills us with laughter and joy. Name your marvelous, quirky, special-to-you delights.

_____

_____

_____

_____

_____

_____

_____

_____

_____

_____

_____

_____

_____

Sometimes we don't see the light of certain mercies and delights until we've walked through seasons of darkness. What hard seasons has God walked you through? And what graces were there to light your way?

_____

_____

_____

_____

_____

_____

_____

_____

_____

_____

_____

_____

_____

_____

_____

_____

_____

We have another fifty days in front of us, and I'm so glad to be on this journey with you. How is it going? Do your routines feel more settled and your days more grounded in God? Think on what changes have been good and perhaps what more could be made.

_____

_____

_____

_____

_____

_____

_____

_____

_____

_____

_____

_____

_____

_____

_____

_____

_____

_____

Divinity can be found in the ordinary.

WEEK

11

A Prayer for Grace

My cup overflows with blessings.

PSALM 23:5 NLT

As we enter our next ten weeks, I offer a prayer for our coming days together:

Heavenly Father, I want so many things right now. A brand-new white leather purse. A spotless home. Maybe even new curtains for the living room. I want so much that doesn't matter in the grand scheme of things. But through my world-colored glasses, I crave a life, an image, and a look that I do not currently have. Forgive the ways I covet more and more and more. Forgive me for lacking gratitude for all that I have, tangible and intangible.

Create in me a desire for that which isn't of this world. Create in me a thirst for Your Word, for Your truth, for time in Your presence. Remind me that whatever I treasure is what my heart longs for. Help me to remember and to treasure that which I cannot see. Help me to see You in the small things and be a vessel of Your love to those around me.

I crave these things of the world because I am broken. Because I think all might be better if I have the perfect look, the perfect house, the perfect image. Make me a reflection of You instead. I lay my earthly worries at Your feet. And I praise You that my cup runneth over.

 Take note of how God reveals Himself in intangible ways today. A hug from a child, a call from a friend, a moment of grace in the evening.

The Keeping of Home

*Protect, through the Holy Spirit who dwells in us, the
treasure which has been entrusted to you.*

2 TIMOTHY 1:14 NASB

When I was writing my second book, *A Simplified Life: Tactical Tools for Intentional Living*, I scribbled the word *homekeeping* on a napkin. The word always made me think of the 1950s *Leave It to Beaver* mom. You know the one: she had a pot roast in the oven and wore heels and lipstick when her husband returned home from work every day at six o'clock. I giggled at the thought but then decided to break down the word a little more.

I discovered that the keeping of home is a beautiful thing. To create a space that is welcoming, warm, cozy, comforting, and rich with love—what an opportunity. It is, for certain, my favorite part of my job as a wife and mother. I've always felt that home is home base. It's where we return. It's where we take off the heavy coats of worry and fear, where we lay down our broken hearts and are simply and fully known. By keeping homes like these, we create the perfect atmosphere for teaching, sharing, learning, worshipping, and growing—a faith-filled, love-filled gathering place. A slice of heaven, if you will.

Prayerfully walk through your home today. Consider how each room is used to bring glory to God. How might you invite God into your home even more? An open Bible on the kitchen counter? A blanket gently placed on a couch for guests? An uplifting song on the radio when the kids come home from school?

Small Things, Big Love

Cast your cares on the LORD and he will sustain you;
he will never let the righteous be shaken.

PSALM 55:22 NIV

Some days are just a race to a finish line. One endless, seemingly meaning-less task after another. A phone call from school. An email that needs sent. A plumber who needs called. It feels as if nothing is actually getting done. When these tasks pile up, I often try to see how much I can fit into a short amount of time. I drop the kids at school and hit the ground running, clock ticking until pickup.

On these days, I find it really important to pause before I dive in. To remind myself that the mundane work I do, the things I have to take care of for our home and family, they matter. To see value in the mundane, to continue working with excellence and diligence through our earthly tasks, is to be obedient to the Lord. And so we prioritize, we make the lists, we handle the things. May you put forth the effort today to find joy and importance in the menial. May the Lord fill you with strength to complete your tasks with a happy heart.

The Lord hears our prayers. He comes before us and behind us. He knows our thoughts before we think them. Nothing is a surprise to Him. Bring your honest thoughts to Him as you go about your day today, reflecting on the big and small things that require your attention and His help. Pray for excellence in the work you do, the emails you send, and even the faucets you fix.

Small but Mighty

*He put another parable before them, saying, "The kingdom of
heaven is like a grain of mustard seed that a man took and sowed
in his field. It is the smallest of all seeds, but when it has grown
it is larger than all the garden plants and becomes a tree, so that
the birds of the air come and make nests in its branches."*

MATTHEW 13:31–32

The Bible says a lot about small things, demonstrating their worth and power in great ways. God sent His Son in the form of a baby, born in a manger, not a king born in a palace (Luke 2). In Matthew, the kingdom of heaven is compared to a mustard seed, the smallest of seeds that grows into the largest of garden plants (13:31–32). The book of Mark tells us that Jesus took note of a poor woman who gave only two coins in an offering—*all* she had, compared to the wealthy who offered only part of their wealth (12:41–44). In John 6, Jesus used a little boy's small lunch to feed five thousand people (vv. 9–13).

What can we learn from these stories of greatness, exponential growth, generous giving, and extraordinary brought forth from the ordinary? God continually does great things through ordinary people and ordinary things. Our modern world constantly tells us we're not enough. We despair over our unworthiness, our regularity, our basic-ness. But God. He does not see us through modern world-colored glasses. Divinity can be found in the ordinary.

 Say a prayer for the small acts of service you will or have completed today. Ask God to create in you a heart of gladness for these ordinary tasks so that they may honor Him and His creation.

The Maker of Lunch

"Here is a boy with five small barley loaves and two small
fish, but how far will they go among so many?"

JOHN 6:9 NIV

The other day my oldest son offered to make lunches for himself and his brother and sister. I think he just wanted extra cookies, but I didn't second guess the favor. Early in the school year, I love making lunches. I cut little shapes out of ham and cheese. I slice apples and soak them in lemon water. I write encouraging notes to each child and buy special "back-to-school" themed napkins.

And then midyear hits (sometimes sooner). Between homework and laundry and work, my excitement for this repetitive act of service has gone stale.

The other day, I read John 6. In this passage we learn of Jesus going to the far shore of the Sea of Galilee. There, hearing of the miracles He'd performed, a crowd of five thousand men followed Him, and Jesus wanted to feed them. Philip, one of Jesus' apostles, declared that it would take half a year's wages to give them each a bite. Another disciple, Andrew, pointed out a little boy with a small lunch: five loaves of bread and two fish. From that lunch, Jesus was able to feed all five thousand men *and* still ended up with twelve bags of leftovers.

Yes, the miracle of what Jesus did with that lunch is incredible. And yet, I smiled at the idea that earlier in that little boy's day, a mother made his lunch.

 What small act of service and love has God used in your life? A seat
belt we remembered to buckle. A text we sent to a hurting friend. A
lunch we made in love.

Reflection

The big things in life are fun. Amazing, really. Weddings. Babies. Big vacations. Career changes. I love those things, and I crave the freshness of their newness and excitement. But the older I get, I've also come to realize that what makes a *good* life often happens in the ordinary and small, the things I can embrace every single day.

What small graces are you thankful for? What small things can you embrace in a big way this week?

_____

_____

_____

_____

_____

_____

_____

_____

_____

_____

Jesus Christ,
Son of God,
have mercy
on me.

WEEK

12

———

A Coffee Date

I have loved thee with an everlasting love: therefore
with lovingkindness have I drawn thee.

JEREMIAH 31:3 KJV

Hi, friend. I think it's time for a coffee date. Pull up a chair. Grab a cup of tea or a mug full of coffee. I want to see how you're doing. Have these recent days been hard? Incredible? Or somewhere in between?

Whether they've been the worst, hardest days of your life or the absolute best, most joyful ones, I wanted to sit with you for a moment and simply remind you that God loves you.

Today, I invite you to take delight in the love of a Father who absolutely, positively loves you. Who knows your heart in its entirety and loves you endlessly.

I placed Jeremiah 31:3, from the *King James Version* of the Bible, here on this page because the poetic translation is so beautiful. *I have loved thee with an everlasting love.* As you consider God's unfailing love for you, let it fill your soul with hope for your future. And I don't mean for the next thirty years of your life—yes, do that, too, but also look just a few days ahead and trust that God is walking both with and ahead of you. And He loves you.

How are you doing? What are you learning? What beautiful thoughts or quotes or words have you collected? What hope do you have for life in the coming season? Is God the source of that hope?

DAY 57

Light to the Darkness

For all have sinned and fall short of the glory of God.

ROMANS 3:23

Deep inside many of us lies a secret. Maybe it's a memory. A regret. An unsettled fear. An addiction. A dream unrealized. A hope we dare not bring to the light of day for fear it may disintegrate. These sacred, tiny parts of ourselves are often buried into the darkest corners of our hearts. They have roots that reach through our hands into the work we do, into our brains and the choices we make, and through our mouths into the words we speak. Everything we do is tinted by these things, whether we realize it or not. In darkness they feed and fester. In light they either blossom or bloom and die.

You may not be ready to bring light to that corner of your heart. But perhaps, instead, let us acknowledge its existence, creating space for it on the outside, when it is ready to emerge. If this is you, I'd like to pray a prayer with you today.

Father, You see all. Nothing inside us, around us, or behind us is hidden to You. Bring Your gentle, healing light to my darkness, to the thoughts I dare not share, the worries I dare not speak, the dream I dare not actualize, the thing I dare not acknowledge for fear that it may break me. Further, the fear that it may break the world's expectation of who I am. I am broken, in a broken world. But I believe in the redemptive power of prayer and while I cannot yet share my darkness with the world, I share it here with You. Jesus Christ, Son of God, have mercy on me, a sinner.

Remember, friend, God always hears us when we call.

Time Hop

Gray hair is a crown of glory; it is gained in a righteous life.

PROVERBS 16:31 ESV

Sometimes Facebook will show me a memory from my past. A photo will pop up on my screen with the caption "On this day in [insert how many years ago . . .]." Initially, I will notice my thinner frame, my wrinkle-free skin. I'll remember the numbers on the scale from those years and remember *just how much those numbers meant to me.* And then the photo will trigger something inside me to remember my mindset when *those numbers were right where I wanted them to be . . .*

And I'll turn to my mirror and smile. I'm not twentysomething Emily anymore. That girl hadn't yet experienced heartache. She hadn't overcome her struggle with food. She hadn't stared diagnosis, death, and infertility in the face yet. Though my face now has a few more wrinkles, these eyes have seen the births of three children (two at once!), these lips have kissed a husband for fourteen years. Though my pant size is different than it once was, these legs have traveled farther than I ever dreamed. They've carried me while we packed moving boxes, while we carefully placed baby carriers into the car for the first time, and while I read the eulogy at my grandfather's funeral.

Aging isn't easy, inside or out. But I see these Facebook memories with a grateful heart now. Grateful for all the ways I've grown and changed, and all the ways God has shown me where my true worth lies.

 What has your body helped you do? Where has it taken you and how have you changed in the last ten, fifteen, twenty years?

Faithful Friendship

*Therefore encourage one another and build one
another up, just as you are doing.*
1 THESSALONIANS 5:11

A few years ago, I had surgery. It wasn't a huge deal, but it was enough that I was told to rest for a few weeks. Not one to accept or ask for help, I spent the weeks before planning for meals and arranging our calendar, certain I could handle it on my own. You see where this is going.

As the date of the operation approached, I received a text from my best friend. It was a link. To a Meal Train. Clicking the link, I realized she'd rallied our immediate group of friends who'd filled a two-week calendar with promises of lasagna, chicken soup, enchiladas, and more. A drop-off time was scheduled for each day, and everyone had Bryan's cell phone number to let him know that day's meal was on the front porch. I cried. I suddenly felt so loved, so seen, and weirdly, so vulnerable.

I knew I could handle it on my own. I could have powered through. But these lovely friends, with busy lives of their own, stepped up because they love me. Their suppers arrived with brownies, half gallons of lemonade, and handwritten notes. One even had a soft pineapple blanket tucked inside as a get-well-soon gift.

To have a village, to be loved and seen and held in your times of need, there is no greater gift.

 Are you willing to ask for and accept help? This is a skill I'm learning, as a recovering control-obsessed person.

Oh, to Be Like Her

Not that we dare to classify or compare ourselves with some of those who are commending themselves. But when they measure themselves by one another and compare themselves with one another, they are without understanding.

2 CORINTHIANS 10:12

There's this writer I *love*. Her words just *stir* something in me. They unlock and unleash feelings I didn't even know I had. When I read her sentences, I feel seen. Understood. Like they've shined a beautiful, gentle light onto my soul.

I compare everything I write to her work. I long to write like her. I know I can do it sometimes, but I feel like *everything* she writes has been touched by the hand of God. Literally. Clearly she's the writer who sits down at her computer, cracks her knuckles, and births ten thousand words a day worthy of a Pulitzer Prize. She doesn't stare blankly out the window. Or abandon her post to do laundry or take a nap to reset her writer's block.

Obviously, this probably isn't the case. But sometimes, for me, it feels like it is. The way I feel when I read a sentence (that could have taken her a week to perfect) tells me that I am inadequate.

This is all hogwash. My heart knows this. My brain, however, sometimes refuses to believe my idols are human.

 The Lord delights in you, just as you are. You are created in His image to be exactly who He needs you to be. Comparing yourself to anyone else (especially anyone else's best moments or perfected hard work) is dangerous. Who are you idolizing? Carve out your special place in the world, and give God your idols.

Reflection

Is it hard for you to realize that God loves you and delights in you? Sometimes it's easy to spend more time dwelling on our secrets and shortcomings, our aging selves, and our deficits than it is to focus on God's incredible love. On the other hand, sometimes it's tempting to overlook our flaws, our sins, our temptations, and brush things off as *fine*.

I think the thing about God's grace is that it meets us where we are, loves us completely, and both holds us and prompts us to grow. But we find that in the still, quiet places with God and His Word.

For this week's reflection, let's sit with the love of God and see what He's whispering in our hearts.

1. Your view of and relationship to God has a huge, eternal impact. It can also impact the dailiness of your life. How do you view God? Have you been able to see and embrace Him as a loving, forgiving Father?

2. If you believe God loves you, do you *live* like you believe God loves you?

_____

_____

_____

_____

_____

_____

_____

3. What is stillness like for you? Does it come easy, or is it a struggle?

_____

_____

_____

_____

_____

_____

_____

_____

4. Do you ever get the feeling you keep some walls around your heart, both with people and God? How could you start chipping away at those walls?

_____

_____

_____

5. List some areas in your life where God has helped you grow.

_____

_____

_____

_____

_____

6. When you think of God's love for you, what tangible things come to mind?

_____

_____

_____

_____

_____

_____

"Making your ear attentive to wisdom and inclining your heart to understanding."

Proverbs 2:2

WEEK

13

A Mother's Love

Train up a child in the way he should go; even when
he is old he will not depart from it.

PROVERBS 22:6

The closest thing I can imagine to God's love for us is the love of a mother for her children. When we consider that God is our Father, perhaps that comparison isn't too far out in left field. I've never felt anything quite like the love I have for my three kids—Brady, Tyler, and Caroline. Each unique in their own way, to me, they are all that is good in the world. They aren't perfect and they make mistakes, but they are pure and precious.

I would love to see them live their lives full of adventure and joy and love and faith. I pray they have incredible friends, partners who cherish them, and achieve all their goals. I pray they are kind, that they look out for others, and that they stand up for what's right. Always. Perfectly. No tears. No crying. No sadness. No hard times. But we know that isn't the case. Life doesn't work that way. The times in my own life when I've struggled or failed or had my heart broken are the times I was cracked, my pain birthing tenderness, empathy, and compassion. We can't control what our children's paths may hold, but we can teach them how to bandage a skinned knee, how to apologize for their mistakes, and how to turn to God—their Father who loves them—at all times.

If you have children, pray for their resilience and compassion. Pray for children in your family and in your community that God would create in them a spirit of kindness and courage.

Be an Includer

Be kind to one another, tenderhearted, forgiving one
another, as God in Christ forgave you.

EPHESIANS 4:32

As a mother, I often question my efforts. Day after day I wash the dishes, only for the sink to be full again. I prepare the meals, and yet, everyone wants to eat again. I correct and commend and teach my children, but sometimes I feel as if my words are going in one ear and out the other.

When Brady started kindergarten a few years ago, every morning as he got out of my car, I started telling him to "have a good day and be an includer." This was my way of encouraging him to always be on the lookout for the left-out kid. For the girl who was always picked last. Or the boy who sat alone at lunch. I said it to him five days a week, year after year.

One day, he told me he and his classmates were choosing writing partners. I asked who he'd picked, and he named a boy I hadn't heard of before. I asked if this boy was a good writer, if maybe that's why he wanted to work with him. "No," he said. "He has been getting in trouble. A lot of the kids ignore him. I think I could be a good example. A friend."

Be still my mama heart. Not only had Brady learned kindness from these words I'd repeated day after day, but he'd learned leadership as well. That which we do repeatedly shapes our lives, and the lives of others. The small choices we make every day become the moments that make up our lives.

What do you repeatedly do or say? What is the hope you have for this repeated action as it shapes your life and the lives of others?

A Tight Grip

Many are the plans in the mind of a man, but it is
the purpose of the L<small>ORD</small> that will stand.

PROVERBS 19:21

I wonder if God gets a good chuckle every morning as I scurry about, tidying up, preparing everyone for the day, trying my hardest to control every inch of our lives. This is never more obvious than when I go out of town. Now I've gotten better, but I used to type up pages about the kids' schedule, routines, and "how we do things" for Bryan or whoever was staying with them.

Even today, as I write this, I'm out of town, and I sent Bryan a text message: "On Fridays I go to the gas station and purchase three small pieces of candy— one for each child. I make sure they're the same, so there's no argument over who gets what. Then I place them in their seats as a little reward for having a good week." Can you believe Bryan had the audacity to ask if he could make his own little fun Friday surprise? "Of course!" I said. But secretly, I wanted him to stick to my plan.

This is often how I work with God too. If God would just listen to *me*; I have a fantastic plan for everything. I mean, I make planners for a living. It's kind of my thing. Alas, He does not. He makes His own plans. I'm learning to let go, to loosen my grip on the calendar, to set down the to-do list, and to just "be" a little more often—allowing God to take the reins.

 Do you struggle with control? What would it look like for you to let God take the reins?

Car Stories

A cloud overshadowed them, and a voice came out of the cloud, "This is my beloved Son; listen to him."

MARK 9:7

I have found a fantastic, magical place where children will spill their hearts. I hope you are sitting down, because this is something most veteran parents know, but I just learned, now that my oldest is approaching eleven years old.

If you have kids, the next time they are in the car with you, ask them a question. Get the conversation started, and then wait for it. The stories will begin spilling. You'll learn of worries, friendship drama, and maybe even secret crushes. The indirect eye contact, both of your eyes on the road ahead of you, and the lack of options to escape the conversation (you know, since you're in a moving vehicle) make this the prime place for heart-to-heart conversations to happen. If you're lucky, and they have a friend in the car, simply listen. You will learn so much.

Make space for someone today, allowing yourself the opportunity to simply listen.

Forts and Sacred Spaces

My people will live in a peaceful neighborhood—
in safe houses, in quiet gardens.

ISAIAH 32:18 MSG

During long days of distance learning and virtual working in the early days of the pandemic, we had to get creative. We turned our kitchen table into an at-home school. Attempting to bring some joy to the situation, I made name tags for each of our three children's seats. I stocked a rolling cart with paints, markers, scissors, paper, puzzles, and more from around our house. In the center of the table, I put mason jars full of freshly sharpened pencils and crayons.

After virtual school, the kids would run upstairs or outside to play while we worked. They built fort after fort after fort. During the early days of quarantine, they slept in a big fort made of chairs and pillows and every blanket in my house. They slept there every night for an entire month. We never took it down, never disturbed it. We even decorated it with signs and Christmas lights. The kitchen school-table and the fort . . . they were their safe spaces. The sacred spaces where joy could be found, where they could be in control, and where nothing could hurt them.

 Where is your safe, sacred space? Perhaps it's in a chair, next to a reading lamp, in the corner of a cozy room. If you don't have one, could you pull together a few items and create one?

Reflection

Motherhood. It's the best, hardest gift some of us can imagine. If you are a mother, reflect on your journey so far. How has God taught you about Him through your role as a mom?

If you are not a mother but long to be, take it to God. Sit with Him in that hard place.

And if you are not a mom and also don't long to be, that's good too. God can use all of us to love people in powerful ways, to create safe spaces for others, and see Him at work in the world.

I will hold myself to a standard of Grace, not perfection.

WEEK

14

For You, Who Are Exhausted

*The LORD is my shepherd, I lack nothing. He makes me lie down
in green pastures, he leads me beside quiet waters.*

PSALM 23:1–2 NIV

Dallas Willard said, "It was an important day in my life when at last I understood that if Jesus needed forty days in the wilderness at one point, I very likely could use three or four."[1]

And so, a benediction for you, who are past the point of exhaustion, desperate for renewal:

May you accept the bountiful grace God is offering you. May you lay down your lists, your tasks, and your calendar and allow the Creator of the heavens and earth to renew your spirit, to create abundant space within you for peace, calm, and rest.

May your head find the cool side of the pillow, even if for just a few moments. May your heart be filled with a gentle song of praise and hope. May you have the guts to lay all of it, every last ounce of your burden, at the foot of the cross of the One who saves you. You are beloved. And you are not a robot. You are a human being, with a body, and a heart, and a soul that require nourishment and replenishment. You are precious and worthy, even and especially in your moments of weariness.

Find the pillow (even if just for a moment). Hear the song (I love "Oceans" by Hillsong UNITED). Breathe in His abiding love for you. In for four, hold for four, out for four, hold for four. Repeat. This is box breathing.

Let the Dishes Lie

May he grant you your heart's desire and fulfill all your plans! May
we shout for joy over your salvation, and in the name of our God
set up our banners! May the Lord fulfill all your petitions!

PSALM 20:4–5

The sun is setting outside and the pelicans are heading back to their homes. Our usual evening routine involves sports practice, homework, a quick dinner, bath, and bed. But tonight is different. Tonight we have something to celebrate. And so we have dinner with friends. Too many to fit at the table, but we squeeze in. Sides are passed, glasses of wine are topped off, little ones are reminded to eat the green beans, not just the bread and butter. Lights down, candles flickering, acoustic Ben Rector in the background barely audible over delightful laughter and chatter. The dishes can wait till tomorrow.

I am a hostess in my heart of hearts. I love a good gathering but have to remind myself not to drown in the details, to fully enjoy good food and good people. And this is why I let the dishes lie. It's a very "not like me" thing to do, but when I ignore this simple thing, I find myself by the fire with friends, sharing stories of college days, or outside in the Adirondack chairs, looking up at the stars with my husband. It's not often, but sometimes the life-giving choice is putting off the responsible one.

Where can you let loose a little? Loosening your grip of control on situations and events or even your home? Where can you let the joy in front of you replace the task at hand?

A Day Off

And he said, "My presence will go with you, and I will give you rest."

EXODUS 33:14

I invite you to take today off. Yes, you heard me. Take the day off. Maybe not from work or *all* your responsibilities if that's not possible, but I invite you to set down the pressure, lay down the busyness, move your nonvital tasks to tomorrow's list.

Sometimes we get so tied up with what we "must-do" that we forget to look around to see if we're overlooking what we "must-not-miss." So tell me: What does it feel like to set your burdens down? Is there something on your schedule today that you can move to next week? Can you spend some time playing instead of hustling? Snuggling on the couch and watching a movie? Can you pour yourself a warm bubble bath and a cup of tea an hour before bedtime, then crawl into bed for a good night's rest? Care for yourself today. If you were looking for permission, this is it. You are enough. You are worthy. You are beloved.

 Take today off. His burden is light.

Grace, Not Perfection

He said to me, "My grace is sufficient for you, for my power is made perfect in weakness." Therefore I will boast all the more gladly of my weaknesses, so that the power of Christ may rest upon me.

2 CORINTHIANS 12:9

"Grace, not perfection" is a slimmed-down version of a phrase I recited to myself in the earliest days of motherhood. When the laundry was piled high, dinner wasn't planned, and my inbox was full, I felt as if I was failing at everything and not doing anything in my life well. I desperately wanted to be more present in my life and to show up more wholeheartedly rather than always be merely checking things off a task list. I wanted permission to fall short in some areas, while excelling in others.

I had that permission; I just didn't see it from my spot on the couch, one foot rocking a baby bassinet, surrounded by towels waiting to be folded. "From now on," I told a friend on the phone, through tears, "I will hold myself to a standard of grace, not perfection." We know what the perfection part is—to have it all together, to "do it all" like everyone else did (or so it seemed). But that standard simply wasn't working for me.

And so grace. Grace sweeps in when I fall short. Grace allows laundry to be put away tomorrow or the next day. Grace is mac and cheese and easy cleanup. Grace is choosing to rest when my body needs it. This phrase is a pillar in my life. A reworking of how I live life and how I show up.

In what areas do you need to receive grace today? Spend a few moments thanking God for the grace He bestows in the big and small moments.

Reflection Sessions

But all things should be done decently and in order.

1 CORINTHIANS 14:40

Ever so often, typically around the changing of the seasons, I take some time to evaluate how things are going. It's a reflective practice I learned from my mom and dad. To do this type of evaluation, I will typically take a half-day off work, and I go somewhere quiet with a journal and my planner. I start by making a list of things working well and things not working well. The "working well" list is like a little pat on the back, but it also inspires new ideas to help alleviate the pain points. The "not working well" list details the places our family could improve how we function and operate.

During one particular evaluation, I noted that getting the kids out the door to school was a definite pain point. Everyone was rushed. Someone always forgot something. And it was rare that anyone's breakfast dishes were ever put away. But I'd been allowing my kids to sleep until the *very last minute* they needed to wake up. No wonder they forgot to brush their teeth and make their beds. So I made a note: set alarms ten minutes earlier. We backed it up by ten minutes until we found that sweet spot where no one was rushed and everyone was starting their day with a happy heart.

Reflection is so helpful when it comes to tweaking, editing, adding, or removing routines from our lives. What worked for our family when we had tiny babies doesn't necessarily work as well now that the kids are older. The coming pages offer some space for your own reflection session; try to schedule some time for it soon—it's a tangible way to incorporate more grace and rest into your life.

WEEK 14

Reflection

This week I talked a lot about rest, time off, and grace. Those things don't always come easy to us. Sometimes we just need an immediate day off, and sometimes we need to take the time to plan for those things. Look at your yearly calendar. Your time off. The rhythms and routines of your months, weeks, and days.

As you have your own reflection session, think through some of these questions:

- What can you quit?
- When can you plan time off?
- Where are your pain points? How can you tweak them?
- What do you need to add to fill your days with more rest and joy?

Don't forget that part of rest is play. Sometimes what we need even more than sleep is joyful connection, laughter, and fun.

Our words
have the power
to move
people.

WEEK

15

Beloved Blankets

Bear one another's burdens, and so fulfill the law of Christ.

GALATIANS 6:2

When my daughter, Caroline, was two years old, I decided to take her to North Carolina to visit my best friend and her newborn twins. She was so excited to fly on an airplane, and I was so excited to have some solo time with my girl. I meticulously packed her mermaid suitcase with everything she'd need, including her beloved pink blanket. It was a small thing, worn and tattered from love, but it was as soft as could be. The plane ride was just a couple of hours, and she happily snuggled up with her blanket and played games.

We landed in Raleigh full of excitement and anticipation, grabbed our bags, and headed to our rental car. And that's when I realized it. The pink blanket was gone. We scoured the airport and called lost and found, to no avail.

By the time we got to my best friend's house, a new pink blanket awaited Caroline. Kristin had dug this precious (and very similar) blanket from her daughter's collection, one of many that wouldn't be missed. Caroline was *delighted*. "New pink blanket" is still a favorite, four years later. Caroline (and I) will never forget the kindness that saved the day.

Mercy shows up in different ways. I was devastated not just because Caroline's beloved blanket was gone but because I had failed her. I'd lost her precious favorite thing. Mercy reminded me that day—through friendship and love—about what is eternal and what is not.

 How has mercy presented itself through friends in your life?

To Be Seen

He will turn the hearts of fathers to their children
and the hearts of children to their fathers.

MALACHI 4:6

Bryan's father passed away a few years ago. They had an up-and-down sort of relationship, but he was a good man. When I ask Bryan about memories of his childhood, he tells me of two things: (1) The time his dad took him to Shoney's for breakfast before school and he got an entire plate of cinnamon apples. He then began to chow down . . . only to realize they were beets. (2) The time his dad checked him out of school early to see *Jurassic Park* at the theater. It was just him and his dad and he felt so proud his dad had chosen him, of his four children, to make this memory with.

It's a beautiful thing to be seen by your father. To be acknowledged and respected as an individual. Even though his dad didn't save him from that bite of beets (if you knew Bryan, you'd laugh hysterically at this—he is not a "beet" guy), he did give him a special memory in the form of dinosaurs and popcorn. Sometimes all it takes is letting someone know you see them, which can make all the difference.

Who in your life needs to be seen? Send them a message or an email.
Or, if you're feeling fancy, take them to a movie. Whatever you do, let
them know they are seen and loved by you.

Home Base

"Love your neighbor as yourself."

MATTHEW 22:39 NIV

The world is a heavy, hard, broken place. Sometimes the news can be so disturbing, so concerning, it's hard to know what to do next. Racial injustice, global concerns, climate change, a pandemic . . . there are too many worries to name. We feel helpless and wonder if, outside of our prayers, there's much we can do. We look around at our lives: our spreadsheets, our lunch making, our concerns about tuition and what to bring to the Sunday school potluck, and wonder if any of it matters in the grand scheme of things.

Yet—and I will speak for my home here—there are five humans living in my house. Five humans, two of whom vote and have careers. Three of whom will one day vote, will one day have families and callings of their own. There are five people here who will, at some point in time, go out into the world to do work, to interact with others, and to—in their own ways—effect change. And so let us celebrate home as home base. Let us feed them, let us nourish their bodies, let us teach love and empathy and compassion. Let us nurture inclusivity, activism, and standing up for what is right. Here, within the walls of this house, chicken and rice help to grow the next generation of changemakers. Here, souls are cared for and truth is taught. Here, "love your neighbor as yourself" isn't just a sign on a wall—it's an undercurrent of daily life.

Imagine if we all experienced a little more love at home. That work matters.

 How do you cultivate a spirit of togetherness, love, and grace that will extend beyond the walls of your home one day?

For You, Who Have Been Hurt

Bless those who persecute you; bless and do not curse them.

ROMANS 12:14

Have hurtful words caused you pain? Sometimes strong words point us toward truth, and sometimes they're just pointless and mean. Hateful words cut like a knife because they are baseless, false, and meant to cause pain. I've been on the receiving end of these words. Both in real life and online. And so, this is for you, who have been hurt:

It is true that hurt people hurt people. Those words, be they few or many, say more about the person who said them than they do about you. We live in a world full of pain, some the likes of which we've never experienced and couldn't possibly understand. Just as we lash out at those closest to us when we are overwhelmed, so, too, do others, wherever they presume to have found an easy target. Those words do not define you, nor should they be allowed space inside your heart. Let them move around you, over you, under you, but do not allow them in you. Remember, pain is a lonely place, and those who are hurting sometimes throw knives to bring other people into the pain so that they are not alone. They think it eases their hurt, their jealousy, their anger, their regret. We know this doesn't help them. And so, today, make space for the hurting who are throwing knives.

Inside every angry, bitter, hateful human is a soul crying to be delivered. As He shows grace to us, allow us to show grace to them. Hold space, say a prayer, let the hurtful words fall away.

 Today, pray for someone who has hurt you. Allow your heart to be released from the confines of anger and resentment.

Honey to the Soul

*Gracious words are like a honeycomb, sweetness
to the soul and health to the body.*

PROVERBS 16:24

Our words, be they in a book like this, in a toast at a dinner party, or in a birthday card to a friend—they have the power to move people. To pull them from an ordinary situation into a transparent moment where they feel truly known and recognized on the deepest of levels. Writing words like that requires us to lay down our egos, our pride, and our belief that we have to say things perfectly. Instead, we have to just say the things.

"I see you and all you have on your plate. I know you feel unnoticed. But I notice and I'm grateful for you. You're doing a good job."

"I know it's not easy being thirteen. You are making big choices every day. No one gets them all right. Just keep making one good choice after the other. I respect you so much."

"I hope you know how strong you are. I see it from the outside, in your dedication to your goal, the way you get up and do the things every morning. I'm so inspired by you and am praying for your path."

"Thank you. I'm so incredibly grateful for you and just wanted to say thank you."

 Who will you bless with your words today?

Reflection

How we treat people matters. It matters for today, and I think it can matter for eternity. Today, I'd love for us to think and pray on two things:

1. Who can we pray for and bless with our kind words? A call, a text, a letter. Some actual face time and a pouring of kind words over them.

_____

_____

_____

2. Who have we hurt or mistreated, intentionally or unintentionally? Self-awareness can be a hard, hard thing. But today, let's ask God if there's someone we need to reach out to in love to ask for forgiveness or make some type of amends.

_____

_____

_____

_____

_____

"May the God of hope
fill you with all joy
and peace in believing, so
that by the power
of the Holy Spirit
you may abound
in hope."

Romans 15:13

WEEK
16

Lackluster

The Lord himself goes before you and will be with you; he will never
leave you nor forsake you. Do not be afraid; do not be discouraged.

DEUTERONOMY 31:8 NIV

I have had seasons of incredible joy, seasons of deep sadness, and some melan-
choly seasons in between. As someone who is pretty consistently upbeat and
happy, a hard season doesn't often look like heartbreak or pain. Instead, it feels
like the colors begin to dull. Joy feels a little less exuberant and anger feels
a little less passionate. If you suffer from this kind of depression on a regular
basis, there are many great resources available, and I would urge you to speak
with a doctor or therapist. Sometimes I just have a down season, and it looks
like an averaging of everything. A thin layer of boredom and apathy lies over
what should be beautiful, bright, and full of life.

I've tried many things to emerge from these seasons of lackluster. New projects. Exercise. Even wine (that doesn't work). And what I've found is that God is
pulling me back to Him. These seasons of lackluster are akin to seasons of fran-
tic overwhelm. I've lost my focus, allowing everything around me to fall or rise
to equal importance—it's hard to prioritize when everything feels the same level
of urgent or blah. Both seasons are a result of priority averaging. The way out?
Making space to hear the Lord's will for my responsibilities. A nap. A journaling
session to sort out my thoughts and write my priorities. An intentional edit of
my belongings and commitments. Grace, upon grace, upon grace.

Have you felt this way? Perhaps you feel this way today? If so, schedule
time to fill your cup, take your thoughts to Him—however blah they
may be—and reprioritize.

Revolutionary, Stubborn Hope

*May the God of hope fill you with all joy and peace in believing, so
that by the power of the Holy Spirit you may abound in hope.*

ROMANS 15:13

When I was pregnant with Brady, the doctors warned me he might not live past birth, if he even survived that long. Then they warned me he might live, but it would be a life that looked vastly different than what we'd hoped and prayed for our son. Upon hearing these dire warnings, I fell apart. But only for a moment. I learned to live what my friend Annie F. Downs calls a "yes . . . and" life for the remainder of my pregnancy.

Yes, I was thrilled to finally be pregnant. Yes, this baby was a blessing no matter what and an answer to so many prayers. Yes, I would and did love him with my entire being. . . . And my heart was broken. I was afraid. I'd never been so afraid, actually. I desperately longed to be in control.

Anne Lamott once said, "I heard a preacher say recently that hope is a revolu-tionary patience; . . . Hope begins in the dark, the stubborn hope that if you just show up and try to do the right thing, the dawn will come. You wait and watch and work: you don't give up."[1] And so I chose hope. I chose to hear the doctors and still hope—not just for my son's health and survival but for the experience of childbirth, for the mark he would make on the world. I hoped for medical miracles, and I also hoped for redemptive love. For God to hold me dear. And though I suffered, He did not leave me alone. My hope was stubborn—His love for me was revolutionary.

 When have you chosen that stubborn, patient hope during a "yes . . . and" situation? How did God walk alongside you through that?

Layers Upon Layers

Am I now trying to win the approval of human beings, or of
God? Or am I trying to please people? If I were still trying
to please people, I would not be a servant of Christ.

GALATIANS 1:10 NIV

As I approach forty, I find myself slowly removing my layers. It's like setting down a cardigan, pulling off one shoe, then another. I imagine that this exercise will not, in fact, leave me naked, but will reveal the very truest, most authentic version of myself, clothed.

We wear a lot of layers in our teens, twenties, and thirties. I can only speak to those decades of adulthood, because those are the only ones I've lived. We wear layers of jealousy, of comparison, of shame. Like a chameleon, we take on the words, beliefs, and style of the people we're around on any given day. We morph a bit when we need to—a little louder here, a little quieter there. Part of this is developing discernment and proper social skills, but part of this is a skill that doesn't serve us at all.

I hear my forties, fifties, and sixties are going to be incredible. And so I am vowing, every single day, to continue to consider my layers, how many I have on, and why I am wearing them. The truest version of myself is probably wearing leggings and a T-shirt.

 Who are you at your most authentic? Underneath all your layers and
fears of rejection, comparison, judgment, and being not enough or too
much—who are you? You're made in God's image, you know, which
makes you pretty special right off the bat.

DAY 79

Before and After

"I the Lord do not change."

MALACHI 3:6 NIV

There are days in life that separate the before from the after. Events that take place that seem to slice through time, pushing a stake down into the soil of our lives, delineating time before this event and time after. We are never the same in the after as we were in the before. Sometimes these events are wrought with loss and deep pain, and sometimes these events are like wings of hope pulling us into some future we could have never imagined.

The loss of a loved one, the start of the pandemic, September 11. Where we were and what we were doing when we heard the news—these details of a moment etched into our memories forever. Writing on the stake indicating "I was here" when it all changed. And so we honor both sides of the path, drawing strength from our unchanging God in an ever-changing world.

Remember the most significant before-and-after in your life. How did it change you? What strength have you carried with you since then?

Winding Roads

He knows us far better than we know ourselves, knows our pregnant condition, and keeps us present before God. That's why we can be so sure that every detail in our lives of love for God is worked into something good.

ROMANS 8:27–28 MSG

I've prayed for a few things that never came to be. Looking back, I'm glad God knew better than I did on those. He saw the big picture, the entire road, whereas I saw just to where the road bends. Perhaps you've had unanswered prayers as well. The engagement that fell apart. The job you didn't get. The person you desperately wanted to notice you.

In the thick of wanting, of knowing *for sure* in all our human capacity, what is best for ourselves, we only see from here to the corner. We can't see the cars that may run the stop sign, the deer that may dart in front of our cars, or the endless bumps that may make a certain journey one not suited for us. And so we trust, and we travel, and we yield when God tells us to wait. We stop when He says it's not our time. Until one day, we look around, and He's brought us home, to all He had planned for us from the beginning. Perhaps it looks like a different destination than we'd imagined. But it's home, and it's perfect for us.

 Remember an unanswered prayer that you're grateful for now. What have you learned since then?

Reflection

Life can be a lot, friend. Sometimes it's abounding in joy and absolute goodness, and sometimes we need the most revolutionary hope to keep going.

If you're going through a season that is lackluster or downright hard, I want you to feel seen today. If I were with you, I'd like to be that friend who hands you a mug of your favorite cozy beverage. The one who wraps you in a hug or squeezes your hand and sits with you in your pain. If you have that person in your life, please reach out to him or her. If you don't right now, I want you to know that God is there too.

1. Whether you're writing here or talking out loud, imagine that God is sitting with you today. What would you tell Him about your pain, your hard or winding roads, and your befores-and-afters? God can handle whatever you need to share.

2. A lackluster day is one thing, but a whole season of it can be downright annoying. Do you have any tips or tricks to get out of it? Do you need to write down your priorities to sort them or simply write ideas to help you feel better? Use this page however you need to.

_____

_____

_____

_____

_____

_____

_____

_____

_____

_____

_____

_____

_____

_____

Layers. Isn't there something kind of freeing about throwing them off and finding your truest self? Though our bodies are changing and aging, I think it's actually an incredible gift for God to grace us with wisdom for our mistakes, empathy for others, and comfort with the skin we're in.

3. So let's talk about layers. These can be actual layers—tangible things in our lives that we love—or metaphorical layers. What things don't quite fit anymore? What needs to be tossed or replaced? And what, my friend, has stood the test of time, that is part of the truest you?

The tiny choices we make every day make up our lives.

WEEK
17

Permission to Say No

God gave us a spirit not of fear but of power and love and self-control.
2 TIMOTHY 1:7

If you're looking for permission to say no, this is it.

As women, we are programmed to be natural caregivers, to live in service of others: our children, our spouses, our communities. But this is a heavy load to carry sometimes, and it often brings about the feeling that we must sacrifice ourselves for the good of others at all times, at all costs. No one knows this better than a mother caring for a small child or an adult child caring for an aging parent.

Some responsibilities in life require dedication and sacrifice for a season, like the ones mentioned above. But some responsibilities are not always ours to carry. And to those, it is okay to say no. Saying no to something isn't just about declining an offer or opportunity, but rather *choosing* to make space for what is more—even if the opportunity we are declining is a seemingly good one. By doing this, we honor what matters most.

In my life I have declined certain professional opportunities to honor more impactful work. I have sometimes said no to get-togethers with friends in honor of a quiet night at home with my husband. I've even declined to enroll my kids in certain sports that require a ton of travel and practices in honor of time together as a family. During other seasons, these yeses and nos have been flipped on their heads. As our priorities shift, so do our yeses and nos.

 Give yourself permission to say no to something today. To cancel a plan, to turn down an invitation, or to politely decline an opportunity in honor of what matters more to you right now.

Set Yourself up for Success

So I run with purpose in every step. I am not just shadowboxing.

1 CORINTHIANS 9:26 NLT

"I wish I were the type of person who woke up at 6 a.m. to work out every day."

I have said these words many times in my life. I've even done it a few times. But the habit never sticks because I inevitably end up choosing to hit Snooze on my alarm.

Then I hear of a friend consistently waking up a few days a week to exercise and I think, *I wish I were like that. I wish it were easier for me.* The truth of the matter is that it's probably not any easier for her than it is for me. She just chooses to make her morning workout a priority. I am choosing sleep and Netflix the night before.

I've begun to realize morning workouts start with my evening routine. They begin when I lay out my workout clothes for the next morning and fill a bottle of water. They begin when I choose to go to bed a little earlier rather than watching television. It seems like a lot of work to prepare for a morning work-out, but by setting myself up for success, I'm more likely to develop the habit I'd like to have—and in the long run be the kind of woman I'd like to be.

How can you set yourself up for success tomorrow morning? Perhaps you don't aspire to be a morning exerciser. Perhaps you'd love to have a cup of coffee waiting on you when you wake up. Think ten steps before that glorious moment when you see that the self-timer you set to brew coffee for you right before you woke up. Make a plan you'll be grateful for tomorrow.

Delight in Discipline

For the moment all discipline seems painful rather than pleasant, but later it
yields the peaceful fruit of righteousness to those who have been trained by it.

HEBREWS 12:11

Have you ever adopted a new habit—say, eating healthy—and given it up after exactly forty-eight hours because you didn't notice an enormous change? It takes a lot of willpower and intention to make healthy choices for two whole days in a row. So why aren't we back in our jeans from college after all that effort?!

I sometimes struggle with maintaining discipline for the long haul. I love immediate gratification, great transformation, and awe-inspiring befores-and-afters. But people who've achieved such things will tell you they only got there by making a series of small choices over and over again for a long period of time.

Let's use vitamins as an example. If I take my vitamins daily for three days, I probably won't see a fantastic impact. I probably won't see a fantastic impact if I take them for a week. But months or even a year? That daily choice will add up to something really good for my body.

The tiny choices we make every day make up our lives. What will you commit to? Moving your body every day? Spending time with God? Wearing sunscreen? Delighting in discipline can be tough, but the long-term rewards are worth it.

 What healthy daily habits would you like to implement? Make note
of one or two. Consider a physical reminder to help you remember
this task. Put a Post-it Note on your bathroom mirror or set up an
automatic reminder notification on your smartphone.

From the Mouths of Babes

Lead me in your truth and teach me, for you are the God
of my salvation; for you I wait all the day long.

PSALM 25:5

Emily Ley Is a Bad Cook has been the title to the book of my life for as long as I can remember. And perhaps, for a little while, it was true. For years I cooked only because the people I lived with and cared for had to eat. I was so busy growing a business and tending to small children, cooking was just a task I had to accomplish, much like putting away laundry. Because I didn't prefer the task over other things, the joke got started.

And it stuck. And I allowed others and myself to believe that Emily Ley Is a Bad Cook. I'd spy recipes that looked delicious and talk myself out of making them because Emily Ley Is a Bad Cook. I'd opt for bakery cupcakes instead of home-made for birthday parties because—you guessed it—Emily Ley Is a Bad Cook.

But one day, my youngest son, who was shoveling baked salmon into his mouth as quickly as he could, said (mouth full), "Mom, you're the best cook." And it was then that a six-year-old stripped me of my long-held title. I looked at my plate and realized I actually was a good cook. For years I'd believed a lie that was rooted in nothing.

I'm still a bit of an apathetic chef in the kitchen, but I've found my work-arounds, and I honor my new title: *Emily Ley Is a Pretty Good Cook.*

 What lie have you written or allowed the world to write on your heart? How might you combat those lies in your heart?

Living Proactively

*You were once darkness, but now you are light in the
Lord. Live as children of light (for the fruit of the light
consists in all goodness, righteousness and truth).*

EPHESIANS 5:8–9 NIV

How do we intentionally clothe ourselves in the Holy Spirit? We do this by choosing the fruit of the Spirit time and time again. When a little one spills her cereal on the kitchen floor, we respond patiently, reminding her that accidents happen and demonstrating how to clean the mess. When we receive a harshly worded email from a coworker, we choose to see the situation from his or her point of view and select kind words in our reply. When our tasks at home mount and our frustration begins to surface, we choose to serve our families with faithfulness out of gratitude to God for His faithfulness toward us.

Making these choices moment after moment is not easy. But by preparing our hearts to reflect the goodness of God, we make space for these choices to happen. This is living proactively versus living reactively. When we begin our days frazzled, overwhelmed, and running on empty, we are reacting to everything life throws at us. But when we set our intentions for the day or the season, asking God to fill us with the fruit of the Spirit no matter what may come our way, we create a plan for how we will respond to the unknowns.

 Choose one fruit of the Spirit to focus on today. For example, if you choose goodness, you may intentionally decide to spend extra time listening to a friend over coffee, helping a coworker with a project, or teaching your children about God's goodness.

Reflection

Saying no, being proactive, delighting in discipline. . . . These can be hard things, friend. But with God, all things are possible. Rather than focus on *all of these things* today, let's just offer up a prayer for the Holy Spirit to move in us. To search our hearts. To intervene for us and help us with whatever it is we need the most today. Feel free to use this space to pray.

Nothing was wasted in the making of who you are.

WEEK

18

The Good Life

So I commend the enjoyment of life, because there is nothing
better for a person under the sun than to eat and drink and
be glad. Then joy will accompany them in their toil all the
days of the life God has given them under the sun.

ECCLESIASTES 8:15 NIV

Somewhere along the way, we develop this idea of what "the good life" looks like. And in our quest to achieve it, to put all the puzzle pieces into precisely the right place, we find that we come up frustrated. We've allowed society, media, and other people to tell us that joy is simply on the other side of XYZ. When you have enough money. When you fit into the right-size jeans. When your children behave exactly a certain way. When your home is completely spotless forever and ever. When you've achieved that goal. And yet, how, exactly, do we get there?

We don't. When we subscribe to this ideal—that when everything is perfect, we'll finally be happy—we'll never actually get there. Instead, we'll spend all our days scurrying, tidying, correcting, toiling, and lamenting the life we still can't quite put together.

The good life is sweet, slow, and flawed. It's lazy Saturday afternoons. A kid who learned to tie his shoes. Time in the garden, pulling weeds long overdue. A hand to hold when bad news comes. Little girls' feet in dress-up shoes far too big. It's a broken lamp and a football-carrying boy saving his allowance. It's bedtime prayers, cups of tea, and Mom's potato casserole.

Write your definition of your own good life, remembering the precious moments that make it up. What ideals do you need to release?

Flamingos and Narwhals

*Yet you, LORD, are our Father. We are the clay, you are
the potter; we are all the work of your hand.*

ISAIAH 64:8 NIV

The same artist who created bright-pink flamingos, vibrant-orange sunsets, narwhals with their underwater horns, and people capable of dreaming up stories like Harry Potter, also created you.

Considering this, I wonder, then, if perhaps all your quirks aren't accidental or weird, but instead if they are intentional and wonderful? How creative and purposeful God must be to have made billions of people, each one special in a million different ways.

To think that He cared enough about me and you—about our communities and our world—to give us each unique gifts, talents, interests, features, and more. How incredibly delightful.

*What makes you unique? Sometimes our quirks are actually arrows
pointing us toward something God has in store for us.*

You and Your Hats

In Christ Jesus you are all sons of God, through faith.

GALATIANS 3:26

You are not defined by your hats. Not by your professional hat or the number of initials that follow your name. Not by the hats you wear as mother, wife, or daughter. Nor are you defined by the hats of your past, even those you regret wearing. No, you are defined by the God who breathed life into you, who created you as perfectly and imperfectly unique as can be. Your definition is one of glory and grace, created and placed within you by the One who went before you, who made a way for you first. Yes, all those hats are wildly important, but above all of them, you are the precious, beloved daughter of the King of all kings.

It's worth noting, of all your hats, that there are some you have the option to change when you're ready. From red to blue, from professional to personal, from cowgirl to derby. I know, you're giggling at my hat analogy, but recently I gave myself permission to evolve. To become a different version of Emily than I was ten, five, even one year ago. My heart as a child of a loving God remains, but my interests, my focus, even my profession can change. And so can yours.

What hats do you wear? Are you defining yourself by one or more of them? Is it time to consider changing hats to best suit who you are today or who you are becoming?

Tell Your Stories

Now we see in a mirror dimly, but then face to face. Now I know in part; then I shall know fully, even as I have been fully known.

1 CORINTHIANS 13:12

I'm learning that our stories make us who we are. Being able to remember them, regretting some, romanticizing others, but retelling them all the same is such a beautiful thing. I invite you to share your stories. Just as nothing was wasted in the making of who you are, no story of yours is meaningless either. You may have enormous up-and-down waves of stories to retell, or you may have a slower trickle of growth and becoming. Whatever your stories, they are precisely that: yours.

Being a writer has taught me to look at life through the lens of constant reflection. Throughout the day, I'm always putting pieces together, searching for meaning in everyday moments, in tales told to me, and in the natural world all around us. It's a beautiful thing to be a gatherer of stories, a collector of meaningful moments. Whether you write about them, journal them, photograph them, film them, or even sing about them, capture your stories. They are the pages of the book you're living each and every day.

 What stories have punctuated your life thus far? Reflect on one particular story, painful or beautiful as it may be. Remember that your stories made you who you are.

An Apology

Do you not know that your bodies are temples of the Holy Spirit, who is in you, whom you have received from God? You are not your own; you were bought at a price. Therefore honor God with your bodies.

1 CORINTHIANS 6:19–20 NIV

I think I owe my body an apology. For all the times I've judged her, wishing she was more or less of herself. For all the times I've deprived her. Mostly, for all the times I didn't listen to her.

She told me what she needed, and I gave her something else, or nothing at all.

The photoshopped magazine models and Instagram squares with all their filtered figures tell us that our bodies are wrong. And that we aren't to trust our bodies. She's too much. She's not enough. She's too soft, too needy.

And yet, this body of mine, she's strong. She's done incredible things. She's changed sizes and shapes. She's grown children. She's developed trust, knowledge, a sense of humor. She's been broken—her right arm, her left wrist, and her heart a couple of times. And she's put herself back together again. She's carried *me*.

What kind of magic is this that my body can do? And why do I shame her so much? Lord, thank You for this body of mine. Help me listen to her and honor her exactly as she is.

 How has your body changed over the years? What magic has she done? Today, I invite you to honor her, exactly as she is, with a reflection of gratitude for all she's gone through with you.

Reflection

If someone hasn't told you recently how unique and wonderful and special you are, I'd like to tell you that today. You're incredible. Deeply known. And so beloved.

Life is not perfect, and we're not perfect. And that's why, in His infinite mercy, God sent Jesus. To forgive us, to hold us, and to fill us with delight. Whether we're switching out our hats and trying to figure out who we are, or we're lamenting over gray hairs and wrinkles, God sees us. God sees you. And He loves you.

> Today, let's take a minute and think through what "the good life" is to us and what some of our favorite little quirks about ourselves are. I think in His infinite wisdom and delight, our quirks can be part of what makes up the good things we treasure the most.

What hats are you wearing right now? Are you hanging on to some that maybe don't quite fit anymore? Or did you toss one long ago that you should have hung on to? As you pray today, ask God to help you bravely evolve into the woman He made you to be.

_____

_____

_____

_____

_____

_____

_____

_____

_____

_____

_____

_____

_____

_____

_____

Write down one of your stories today. Something that makes you belly laugh or a time when God showed up in your life in a big way. Write a story you want to always remember and pass along.

_____

_____

_____

_____

_____

_____

_____

_____

_____

_____

_____

_____

_____

_____

_____

_____

_____

_____

_____

_____

The good life
is sweet,
slow, and
flawed.

WEEK

19

You Are Here

Even when I walk through the darkest valley, I will not be afraid, for you
are close beside me. Your rod and your staff protect and comfort me.
PSALM 23:4 NLT

You are not lost. It may feel like the compass is spinning and you aren't sure which way is north, but you are not lost. You are exactly where you are. Feel your feet planted on the ground. Feel your heart beating inside your chest. Feel the air fill your lungs as you breathe.

You are here. You are not lost.

Look around you, at the handle on the mug, the coffee drips on the side. See the books on the table: an old favorite, with its worn edges and dog-eared pages. A recent purchase, with its shiny dust jacket.

You are here. You are not lost.

When tragedy strikes. When the bad news comes. When another breaking-news ticker scrolls across the screen, remember: you are here.

You are beloved. You are capable. And you are not lost. God has told us He will not forsake us. And though we may walk through the valley of the shadow of death, He will remain by our side.

 Allow the details of your life to center you and ground you, when everything else feels unstable. The next time you feel lost, look around. You are here.

Self-Care Is Not Selfish

Dear friend, I pray that you may enjoy good health and that all may go well with you, even as your soul is getting along well.

3 JOHN 1:2 NIV

There is nothing more urgent than caring for yourself. Today I invite you to evaluate how you're doing. What is working for you right now? What isn't working? What in your life is lacking or lagging and needs your attention?

You are the only person who knows what you need. Perhaps you need help. Perhaps you need time. Perhaps you need rest. Whatever it is, give yourself permission to ask for it and to accept it. We honor God by caring for ourselves, so that we can best reflect Him in the world. When we are running on empty, we aren't able to function at our best. And we all know this world requires a lot from us.

Self-care is not selfish. But self-care doesn't end at a pedicure and a nap. Self-care means caring for ourselves the way we care for others. When my child is sick, I give him or her a warm bath, feed them a nourishing bowl of chicken soup, and tuck them into a warm bed. Caring for a sick child feels so different than the way I care for myself when I am out of sorts. I often push myself forward, telling myself to keep going, when my body is telling me it needs rest and care.

 Whatever your body is telling you today, honor it. And if needed, take a bath, make yourself a cup of soup, and allow your body to rest. Caring for yourself is one of the most selfless acts of service to those around you.

Moving Forward in Faith

*My flesh and my heart may fail, but God is the strength
of my heart and my portion forever.*

PSALM 73:26

I had my heart broken once. I remember going to lunch with a friend, right after my engagement was called off, and staring at my plate—my most favorite chicken salad in town—and not having the energy to pick up my fork. I wanted nothing to eat. All I wanted was for my life to be put back together.

I'd always believed that two plus two equals four. That if I made good choices, did the right things, and followed the right path everything would work out in my favor. Until one day, it didn't. Suddenly two plus two equaled three or thirty-seven or something else that made no sense.

That was the first time I learned that bad things can happen to good people. That there is no perfect equation to always getting what you want. And though I wouldn't truly realize it until more of my story unfolded, sometimes what we think is the best outcome *ever*, pales in comparison to what is coming.

When the path ahead is dark, sometimes all we can do is keep moving forward in faith. Then one day we'll realize God has taken us on a journey far better than the one we had in mind.

 Have your equations and expectations ever fallen apart? Does two plus two somehow suddenly give you an answer you didn't expect?

Middle of the Mess

The grace of God has appeared, bringing salvation for all people.

TITUS 2:11

I've told the story of making a big business decision a few years back so many times I have it memorized. The company I founded, Simplified, had grown exponentially. Our products were carried in eight hundred stores around the world. It was a dream. And I was miserable. With three little ones at home, a full travel schedule, and no time to sleep or be creative, I was maxed out.

We ended up cutting our wholesale program—the majority of those eight hundred stores—and focused on growing our community and online shop. We doubled our revenue. It's a beautiful story. It's cut-and-dried. When I tell it now, it feels like a quick plot: problem, solution; pain, healing; mess, reorganization. But oh, when I was living that story, I was anything but sure. There were tears. A lot of them. And a lot of anguish trying to figure out which path, of seemingly a million of them, was the right one forward.

When we're in the middle of the forest, we cannot see the clearing. When we're in the middle of our stories, we can't fathom how it will end. So often we forget that change and growth happen in the struggle, through the effort, and under the pressure. May we, then, not rush toward quick fixes, but rather allow our struggles to shape us.

How has God used struggle to shape you? As it is often said, hindsight is twenty-twenty. Is there a time in your life when you felt God's hand on your shoulder while you walked an unknown path?

Nothing Is Wasted

But one thing I do, forgetting those things which are behind and reaching forward to those things which are ahead, I press toward the goal for the prize of the upward call of God in Christ Jesus.

PHILIPPIANS 3:13–14 NKJV

One day you're going to look back and realize the pieces were falling into place all along. A piece here, a piece there. When you're in the middle of the puzzle, it's impossible to see all the ways in which you're coming together.

One day you're going to realize you were becoming all along. Through every triumph, every tear, every conversation, every moment of uncertainty. All of those things were shaping you, whittling you into the woman God made you to be.

Nothing was wasted in the making of who you are—no part of your journey, no story, no experience, no gain or loss. Every ounce of your story matters.

 What part of your story do you wish you could erase? How has it impacted who you have become? Has it made you stronger? Wiser? More grounded? Give thanks for the hard-won strength you have.

Reflection

Have you ever felt lost or forsaken? What was that experience like for you? Are you still in the midst of it, or can you start to see ways that God was working during that time?

Here's to the brave ones.

(YOU'RE A BRAVE ONE)

WEEK

20

Eyes on the Horizon

Set your minds on things that are above, not on things that are on earth.

COLOSSIANS 3:2

My friend Whitney is a runner. She inspires me a lot with her dedication to moving her body, knowing it fuels her creativity as a designer and her energy as a mother.

When I struggle with running, she reminds me that if I keep my eyes on the road, analyzing and counting every single step, the run will be much harder. I'll lose my endurance in the details.

Instead, she encourages me: Keep your eyes on the horizon. Pick a point a ways ahead—maybe a tree or a cross street or a building. Focus on that long-term finish line rather than every individual step.

So every time I find myself getting buried in the details, and lost in every tiny step, I lift my chin and focus on the bigger picture: the run itself. Then I'm able to complete the race.

If you're lost in the details of your run today, try picking a point a ways ahead. The completed project, rather than the step you're on right now. The child you're raising, rather than the behavior you're correcting right now. Or the marriage you're cultivating, rather than the argument you had this morning. Chin up. Eyes on the horizon.

Mile Twenty-Two

*Therefore, brothers, be all the more diligent to confirm your calling
and election, for if you practice these qualities you will never fall.*

2 PETER 1:10

When you're a lover of fresh starts, it's hard to stay the course when things feel stale. It's even harder when you were made to be a builder. For years my heart has lit up at the idea of building: building a marriage, a family, a business, a brand, a career. And even on the smaller side—a home, a new website, a new product. But when the adrenaline is waning and the race to the finish line is over, the day-to-day can be hard. Mundane. Building a marriage is exciting, but learning to communicate well isn't that much fun. Building a home is awesome, but emptying the dishwasher is my least favorite chore. Building a business is incredible, but calculating taxes and navigating human resources is not my idea of a good time.

I've heard this is comparable to running marathons. The excitement for the big race is real, and the feeling you have at the finish line is amazing. But on mile seven? And mile twenty-two . . . that's hard. It's the tending and the work that matter. The roses only grew because you watered and weeded them. The business you built only came to be because you put in the late nights and googled until your fingers hurt. My parents, who have been married for forty-seven years, tell me they've only achieved such a milestone because they chose each other over and over again, even when the going got tough.

 What work are you doing in your life, tending your garden to achieve a certain result? Where will the reward be and what are you doing to get there?

Dream in the Light

"I have said these things to you, that in me you may have peace. In the world you will have tribulation. But take heart; I have overcome the world."

JOHN 16:33

What is the dream you dare not say out loud? The one so fragile you keep it wrapped neatly in tissue paper, tucked deep into the corner of your heart so that it may never crack or fade or wilt from the sun. So that it cannot be made fun of, judged, or ridiculed. So no one can ever tell you it has no place in your heart or that it will never come to be.

I invite you to bring it to the light today. To tenderly hold it in front of you and consider what life might look like if you were to allow this dream the space to exist beside you. If you don't have a dream you're considering right now, perhaps you'll allow yourself the freedom to take a creative look at your life. What hopes and dreams have been put on your heart in recent months? Is God inviting you to step into something new or acknowledge a desire He's planted within you?

 Give yourself permission to become tomorrow's version of yourself. Acknowledging the desires of your heart and bringing them to the Lord allows your innermost hopes and dreams to be illuminated.

The Slow Burn

The plans of the diligent lead surely to abundance, but
everyone who is hasty comes only to poverty.

PROVERBS 21:5

Our culture has taught us to celebrate the quick win, the trophy, the work-hard and play-hard mentality. And while it's true that some things can be achieved quickly by pushing hard, staying up late, and giving it all you've got, that's also a recipe for burnout.

Could we, instead, honor the slow burn? The progress made inch by inch, little by little, hour by hour. We might be able to move quickly to win races, but when we move so fast and expect such big results, we miss something. A builder throwing up a house will miss the opportunities to add a window here or finesse the porch just so. A writer rushing through her pages will miss the chance to add those perfect words that will stir a reader's soul in a lasting way. A chef throwing together a bowl of spaghetti for his family might miss the opportunity to simmer the noodles just a few minutes longer to achieve that perfect texture or to mince the basil before adding it to the marinara so the flavor is drawn out just right.

The slow burn is where iron is shaped. Good things take time. Though we can't often see drastic change through the slow process of growing, the before-and-after can be staggering.

 What are you slowly burning? How do you hope to see change when the burn is complete? Is there anything you are rushing and need to slow down?

Here's to the Brave Ones

We have this hope as an anchor for the soul, firm and secure.
HEBREWS 6:19 NIV

We did it, sister. One hundred days of letting God into our mornings and His mercy and delight into our hearts. Today, I raise my coffee mug to you and leave you with this:

Here's to the brave ones. The ones who put one foot in front of the other when life hurts. Who keep fighting, keep going, and keep showing up, even when giving in would be so much easier.

Showing up, after all, is half the battle. Once you've done that much, you're nearly to the finish line.

If you woke up today and put your feet on the floor to face the appointment, the phone call, the conversation, the treatment, or even just another day under the weight of the hidden pain you carry, you've done it. You're here. That step matters.

And you are not alone.

The God who created the heavens and earth and all the beautiful things on it also created you, on purpose, for a purpose. He celebrates your showing up and He is working in you a great work of life, even when you can only take one tiny step at a time. In your stamina, your choice to keep moving, He is pleased. Keep going.

 If all you have in you today is the ability to get out of bed, that is enough. Momentum is momentum, no matter how small. Today, ask God for the strength, energy, and power to keep going.

Closing Thoughts

Let us hold tightly without wavering to the hope we affirm,
for God can be trusted to keep his promise.

HEBREWS 10:23 NLT

Hi, friend! Here we are, wrapping up one hundred days together. Today, I invite you to reflect on all this has held for you. Take inventory and account of where you've been so that you might make tweaks and adjustments to move forward boldly, intentionally, and with gratitude.

UPS: What achievements, big or small, have you made so far?

DOWNS: What stumbling blocks or mistakes have occurred?

_____

_____

_____

_____

_____

_____

_____

_____

_____

LEARNING: Through the ups and the downs, what is God teaching you about Himself and about yourself?

_____

_____

_____

_____

_____

_____

_____

LOOKING AHEAD: What hopes do you have for your next one hundred days?

_____

_____

_____

_____

_____

_____

_____

_____

Considering your answers to these questions, I invite you to spend some time quieting your heart and mind before God. I have a few reminders for you:

- UPS: You have permission to celebrate every victory no matter how private, tiny, or nuanced it might be. Every inch forward is momentum.
- DOWNS: You are not defined by your downs. They are part of the human experience. You are neither too much nor not enough. Grace upon grace.
- LEARNING: You know what He's teaching you, even if it's hard to learn. Lean in. Allow His purpose to unfold, no matter what it may require from you.
- LOOKING AHEAD: Boldly believe in God's promises: God designed you for a purpose (Ephesians 2:10). God will strengthen and help you (Isaiah 41:10). God can be trusted (Hebrews 10:23). Tune into Him and just watch what He'll do over the next six months.

We are his workmanship, created in Christ Jesus for good works, which God prepared beforehand, that we should walk in them.

EPHESIANS 2:10

"Fear not, for I am with you; be not dismayed, for I am your God; I will strengthen you, I will help you, I will uphold you with my righteous right hand."

ISAIAH 41:10

Let us hold fast the confession of our hope without wavering, for he who promised is faithful.

HEBREWS 10:23

And before we go, just a few more things to remember.

God is fully present everywhere.
God is merciful. He shows mercy to us in many ways.
God is faithful. He always keeps His promises.
God is good. He does what is best and can do no harm.

For what He promised, He has fulfilled. Let grace wash over you, delight stir within you, and mercy cover your heart. "For God so loved the world, that he gave his only Son, that whoever believes in him should not perish but have eternal life" (John 3:16).

He is risen; He is risen indeed.

You are beloved. You are chosen. You are invited to sit at the table with Jesus, with all your baggage and questions and doubts. He welcomes you here.

A Prayer of Gratitude

Lord, thank You for the work You are doing in me. For the ways You are knotting me up inside so that I will pay attention. Thank You for pressing in and pushing me on. Thank You for not giving up on me, even when I've all but given up on myself. Lord, I praise You for Your relentless pursuit of me, though sometimes I do not know why You pursue me at all. God, I may fight You off sometimes, but please never stop coming after me. Please continue to put pressure on my pain points, pressing gently into my bruises, and leading my feet onto the fire so that I might discover new spaces and new places You'd have me visit.

Continue to shape me, continue to turn me inside out. When I feel the discomfort rise, the frustration simmer, and my insides begin to stretch, allow me to know that it is You inside me doing what only You can do. Help me to be brave, strong, and steadfast. Help me to lean on You when I feel like I can't take another step. In Your holy name I pray. Amen.

A Benediction

May the Lord meet you right where you are, the past behind you and the future ahead of you. May He plant within you a bold spirit of hope and faith in what's to come, trusting that He is the King of all kings, the Creator of all things, our Miracle Worker.

PS: Next time you're in the shower, turn on the song "Oceans" by Hillsong UNITED. Sing it loud.

Scriptures for Your Morning

Let me hear in the morning of your steadfast love, for in you I trust.
Make me know the way I should go, for to you I lift up my soul.

PSALM 143:8

The Lord's unfailing love and mercy still continue,
fresh as the morning, as sure as the sunrise.

LAMENTATIONS 3:22–23 GNT

For his anger is but for a moment, and his favor is for a lifetime.
Weeping may tarry for the night, but joy comes with the morning.

PSALM 30:5

"Have you commanded the morning since your days
began, and caused the dawn to know its place?"

JOB 38:12

But I will sing of your strength; I will sing aloud of your
steadfast love in the morning. For you have been to me
a fortress and a refuge in the day of my distress.

PSALM 59:16

Satisfy us in the morning with your steadfast love,
that we may rejoice and be glad all our days.

PSALM 90:14

Morning Routines

I've both read and experienced that the way we start our mornings can determine how the rest of the day goes. When our mornings are frenzied, hurried, and stressful, our afternoons typically follow suit. The stress of not having enough time to eat a decent breakfast, looking for the missing shoe that can't be found, or scurrying about collecting jackets and notes and the laptop for work just sets the tone for the rest of the day. (Even typing that gives me anxiety because I can feel that experience in my bones as recent as last week.)

But when I back up ten steps, when I set myself up for morning success (beginning the night before), my morning runs so much smoother. I rise a little earlier so I can make breakfast, the shoes are already set out for the kids, and everything I need for my workday has been collected and is ready to go right next to my purse. I take a deep breath as I pour a cup of coffee from the pot that was set to brew right on time. I have patience for myself and my kids as we go about our routine in a calm, collected way. And I'm able to approach the rest of my day with the same cool, confident attitude.

Granted, no routine is ever perfect. Someone will oversleep. The umbrella will be misplaced. And there won't be enough milk for everyone's cereal. That happens. Developing a tried-and-true morning routine requires equal parts dedication to doing it consistently and grace for when it falls apart.

As you begin to dream up your ideal morning routine, I invite you to think high level (big picture) and low level (very granular). Allow yourself to dream. Do you love Adele? Set your alarm to her music. Do you enjoy a few minutes to journal or reflect in the morning? Arrange a blanket, pen, and your Bible or journal near your favorite chair. Within the limits of your real life (yes, we'd all love to have a personal chef make our breakfasts each day, but alas . . .), how can you create realistic structure and infuse joy as much as possible? I have found it *extremely* helpful not just to dream up my routines but to actually write them down. I even went so far as to write out my morning skincare routine and tape it to my bathroom mirror so that I will stop forgetting my sunscreen!

Set yourself up for success and you will be so glad you did in the morning. And remember . . . His mercies are new with each rising sun. You don't have to do this perfectly, but you are fully capable of doing it consistently and truly changing the quality of your life in the process.

Emily's Ideal Morning Routine

Night before: Pick up living room and kitchen. Set coffee maker up to brew in the morning. Make sure kids have packed lunches and water bottles.

> #1: Hit Snooze a few times, then get up and take a hot bath. Throw on workout clothes.
> #2: Make a cup of coffee and get breakfast ready for the kids.
> #3: Get kids ready for school; enjoy breakfast with them.
> #4: Say goodbye to kids and get in a little exercise.
> #5: Get ready for my day (shower, skincare, vitamins, get dressed).

EMILY'S PAIN POINTS

My kids are pros at oversleeping. We recently bought them all alarm clocks so they can wake up on their own.

Cooking anything takes me too long. So I keep a few easy, healthy breakfast options in my back pocket to avoid skipping breakfast or spending too much time in the kitchen: avocado toast, yogurt and granola, scrambled eggs and avocado (sometimes add in a little chicken sausage). It's also helpful to make a breakfast casserole on the weekends for easy reheated breakfasts for everyone during the week.

I love sleep. I could sleep for ten hours if my schedule allowed. Giving myself grace to hit Snooze a few times helps me slowly wake up.

I won't sacrifice my hot bath. I love that time alone to read for a few minutes and get my mind right before tackling the morning.

EMILY'S IDEAL WEEKEND MORNING

Honestly, we let our kids sleep in and routines fall to the wayside on weekends. Everyone wakes up in their own time (no alarms unless we need to be somewhere). Our kids know how to make their own breakfasts, and the lack of routine makes us all really happy. Lazy Saturdays with my people are fuel for more structured days during the week.

TIPS AND TRICKS TO START YOUR DAY

- Set yourself up for success the night before (put the coffee on auto-brew, run the dishwasher, lay out your workout clothes, or whatever will help you the most).
- When picking up the house in the evening (or morning, whichever you fancy), throw everything that's out of place into a laundry basket to be put away whenever you have time. It's instant gratification and grace in one.
- Get your kids involved in the routines. They'll love taking ownership of their mornings.
- Write. It. Down. Put your morning routine on a piece of paper and tape it to the fridge or to your mirror. Keep it where you can see it so you don't have to waste brainpower remembering which steps you're forgetting.
- Throw a load of laundry in the washer as soon as you wake up. I run mine on the speed cycle to save energy and water—plus it only takes twenty-eight minutes!
- Don't forget to spend some time getting your heart and mind right every morning. Whether it's a few minutes reading a devotional or studying the Bible, a journaling session, or even a quiet morning meditation listing three things you're grateful for, this practice will help you approach your morning and your day with a positive frame of mind.

My Current Morning Routine

Use these pages to work through your current routines and your pain points, and then map out your ideal routines, but remember: focus on equal parts dedication and grace.

My Personal Pain Points

_____

_____

_____

_____

_____

_____

_____

Ideas to Overcome My Morning Challenges

_____

_____

_____

_____

_____

_____

My Ideal Morning Routine

_____

_____

_____

_____

_____

_____

_____

_____

_____

My Ideal Weekend Morning Routine

_____

_____

_____

_____

_____

_____

_____

_____

Acknowledgments

To Bryan, Brady, Tyler, and Caroline. I love you dearly and am so grateful for your love and faith in me.

Mom and Dad, thank you for encouraging me now and as a little girl. Your example is a guiding light.

Team Simplified, you make me better. I couldn't do this work without you.

To my best friends, Jane and Kristin, thank you for loving me and cheering me on even when I have to crawl into my writing cave for a bit. I love you both!

To my literary agent, Claudia, and my Thomas Nelson publishing team, thank you for loving this book into existence. I am so thankful to work with the best of the best.

Notes

Day 2: What Matters Most
1. James Clear, *Atomic Habits* (New York: Avery, 2018), 246.

Day 7: God Meets Us Where We Are
1. Larry Crabb, *Real Church: Does It Exist? Can I Find It?* (Nashville: Thomas Nelson, 2009).

Day 15: Breath of Life
1. "Jesus Prayer-Prayer of the Heart," Orthodox Prayer, accessed February 22, 2022, https://orthodoxprayer.org/Jesus%20Prayer.html.

2. Christophe André, "Proper Breathing Brings Better Health," January 15, 2019, Scientific American, https://www.scientificamerican.com/article /proper-breathing-brings-better-health/.

Day 27: Protect the Asset
1. Greg McKeown, *Essentialism: The Disciplined Pursuit of Less* (New York: Crown Business, 2014), 94.

Day 66: For You, Who Are Exhausted
1. Dallas Willard, *The Divine Conspiracy: Rediscovering Our Hidden Life in God* (San Francisco: HarperSanFrancisco, 1998), 355.

Day 77: Revolutionary, Stubborn Hope
1. Anne Lamott, *Bird by Bird: Some Instructions on Writing and Life*, 2nd ed. (New York: Anchor Books, 2019), xxiv.

About the Author

Emily Ley is the founder of Simplified®, a bestselling brand of planners and organizational tools for busy women found online and in Target, Walmart, Office Depot, and Staples.

She has spent nearly thirteen years empowering, inspiring, and equipping women in the areas of organization, planning, and simplicity. She is the host of The Simplified Podcast and author of national bestselling books *Grace, Not Perfection*; *A Simplified Life*; *When Less Becomes More*; and *Growing Boldly*.

Emily has been featured in *Forbes*, *Glamour*, and *Good Housekeeping* and was recently recognized as Entrepreneur of the Year by Studer Community Institute. She also serves on the board of advisors for the Rally Foundation for Childhood Cancer Research.

Now, as an author, podcaster, entrepreneur, wife, and mother, Emily lives in Pensacola, Florida, with her husband, Bryan, and their son Brady, and twins, Tyler and Caroline.